FROM CHAPEL TO CHIEF CONSTABLE

From Chapel to Chief Constable

Principles, Politics and Public Service

TONY LEONARD

YOUCAXTON
PUBLICATIONS

Copyright © Tony Leonard 2020

The Author asserts the moral right to
be identified as the author of this work.

ISBN 978-1-913425-66-1
Published by YouCaxton Publications 2020
YCBN: 01

All rights reserved. No part of this publication may be reproduced, stored in a retrieval system, or transmitted in any form or by any means, electronic, mechanical, photocopying, recording or otherwise, without the prior permission of the author.

This book is sold subject to the condition that it shall not, by way of trade or otherwise, be lent, resold, hired out or otherwise circulated without the author's prior consent in any form of binding or cover other than that in which it is published and without a similar condition including this condition being imposed on the subsequent purchaser.

YouCaxton Publications
www.youcaxton.co.uk

Two lines of text of 'One more step along the world I go' (Sydney Carter; 1915-2004), © 1971 Stainer & Bell Ltd, 23 Gruneisen Road, London N3 1DZ, www.stainer.co.uk, are used by permission. All rights reserved.

> 'And it's from the old
> I travel to the new.
> Keep me travelling
> along with you.'
> *Sydney Carter*

Acknowledgements

I have been fortunate to have met and worked with many good people over the years, far too numerous to list here, but I do recognise and acknowledge their contribution to both my personal and professional life.

One group stands out, however, without whose love and support I could never have achieved anything - my family. Kathleen has been a tower of strength and has put up with so much that I can never fully express the depth of my gratitude to her. As children, Debra and Stuart coped with having to change schools and leave friends behind, despite not being consulted in advance. As adults, they have shown such consistent love and support which has encouraged us tremendously.

Contents

Chapter One	Home & Early Family Life	1
Chapter Two	What was Storthes Hall?	5
Chapter Three	Infant & Junior School	13
Chapter Four	Highburton Methodist Chapel	18
Chapter Five	National Service	21
Chapter Six	Teaching and Goldsmiths' College	29
Chapter Seven	Joining the Lancashire Constabulary	31
Chapter Eight	Marriage and a new Family	39
Chapter Nine	Post Probationary Policing	41
Chapter Ten	The Special Course, Bramshill	52
Chapter Eleven	London School of Economics & Political Science	57
Chapter Twelve	Return to Lancashire	60
Chapter Thirteen	Promotion to Chief Inspector	66
Chapter Fourteen	Transfer to the Derbyshire Constabulary	70
Chapter Fifteen	Promotion to Assistant Chief Constable	77
Chapter Sixteen	Transfer to Sussex Police	84
Chapter Seventeen	Transfer to Humberside	93
Chapter Eighteen	The Next Step - Retirement	103

Chapter One

Home & Early Family Life

Dad began his training as a student nurse in 1934 at Storthes Hall Mental Hospital, near Huddersfield, where he qualified as both a Registered Mental Nurse (RMN) and Registered Member of the Psychological Association (RMPA). Following their marriage in 1937, Mum and Dad rented number 48 Storthes Hall Lane, Kirkburton, a three bedroomed semi-detached property owned by the hospital. I was born there on 10 March 1939 followed by my sister, Dilys, on 11 November 1943.

My earliest memories are of a house full of people. Mum's younger sister, Gwyneth, also worked at the hospital and lived with us. For most of the war years my cousins Elvet and Philip and Glyn and Olwen, the children of two of my mother's brothers, were voluntarily evacuated from London and Liverpool respectively to join us in the relative peace of the Yorkshire countryside.

Our house had gardens to the front and rear. Vegetables and soft fruits were grown in the back garden, at the bottom of which was an air raid shelter shared with the family from No. 46. The family at No. 50 kept chickens and supplied us with fresh eggs in return for potato peelings and other food scraps used to feed the poultry. I never remember being hungry, but was constantly cold in the winter months when ice would form on the inside of our bedroom windows.

Permanent shortages of coal meant that alternative combustible materials had to be collected from local woodland. During wartime logging operations, whole families gathered the chippings produced by axe wielding lumbermen into hessian sacks as supplementary fuel for their homes. At the age of three, I was almost killed when I ran out in front of a tree as it was being felled and was only saved from death or serious injury because a large branch hit the ground first, preventing the trunk from crushing me.

I always felt loved and secure as a child and our house was a happy home, but as children we were encouraged to accept that adults knew best. My sister and I got on quite well as children despite our age difference, but I do remember one occasion when she must have been about three or four years old. I was playing with friends by the front door and refused to let her join in the game. Dilys went into the house, came out with a hammer from Dad's toolbox and hit me over the head with it. Blood spurted up like a fountain and everyone screamed, not least me. Fortunately the wound was only superficial, but I learned to be careful not to upset her in future.

Dad was conscripted in 1942 into the Royal Army Medical Corps and, after initial military training, was promoted to sergeant because of his nursing qualifications. He served in military hospitals in England and Northern Ireland before taking part in the invasion of Europe. He landed on D2, the second day of the invasion, and helped to set up and staff a field hospital at the beachhead. He was fortunate to escape being killed when a German artillery shell burst through the roof of the hospital tent during an operation but failed to explode. After several months in Normandy he was transferred to a military hospital in Bangalore in India and then to Burma where he was involved in the operation to recover and treat escaped British prisoners of war and troops who had been separated from their units during the Japanese offensive. He finally arrived back in the UK in late 1946, docking in Liverpool, where Mum and I welcomed him home from the troopship 'Empress of India.'

Family Holidays
Although we couldn't go away on holiday during the war years, I remember visiting my uncle Will and his family in Liverpool after Olwen and Glyn had returned home. In the summer of 1944 we were staying with them when an unexploded bomb detonated in their street and many of the windows were shattered. I can still picture the barrage balloons deployed around a nearby power station.

When Dad returned from the army after the war, holidays were mostly spent at the homes of relatives because we couldn't afford to stay in boarding houses or hotels. My very first sight of the sea was at Porthcawl in South Wales.

Our first proper family holiday was to Whitby in 1950, travelling there by bus and changing at Leeds, a journey lasting over six hours. We stayed on a farm in a converted single-deck bus which still had the bells fitted so Dilys and I played buses when it rained and we couldn't go out. Each day Dad would dig a hole to empty the chemical lavatory and we had to carry water in jerry cans from the farm for cooking and washing. It was about a twenty minute walk to the beach at Upgang, between Whitby and Sandsend, which still had remains of anti-landing craft defences. Whitby became our regular holiday destination and we progressed from the converted bus to a proper caravan with more room and better facilities. One of the special treats of the annual holiday was going to the theatre to see a play performed by professional actors from a repertory company.

During the Festival of Britain in 1951 we spent a week in London staying at a Salvation Army lodging house in dormitory accommodation because that was the cheapest Mum and Dad could find. Part way through the holiday Dad had to return home for a promotion interview. Thankfully he got the job and family finances improved. This was the first visit to London for Dilys and me and we were fascinated by everything we saw. One particularly memorable event was getting free tickets from the BBC for a live radio broadcast of "The Goon Show" starring Peter Sellers, Harry Secombe, Spike Milligan and Michael Bentine. I was already a fan of the show and was thrilled to see them all on stage in person reading their scripts into the microphones. We also visited Madame Tussauds, the Science and Natural History Museums. Dilys and I loved the funfair in Battersea Park and travelling on the tube and the escalators at the underground stations.

Getting About

The normal way for us to get around in the 1940s and 1950s was on foot. We regularly walked four or five miles to go shopping without thinking it at all unusual. The bus from the hospital into Huddersfield ran once an hour from Monday to Saturday and every two hours on a Sunday. During my childhood only one family in Storthes Hall Lane had a car and whenever they passed anyone walking home they would be expected to stop and give them a lift, especially if they were carrying shopping.

Bicycles were common among adults and very highly prized by children. When I was ten Dad built my first bike for me from scratch from parts of old bikes he managed to salvage or scrounge. He taught me to ride, how to look after it and how to mend a puncture. I was so proud that in the summer I rode it to and from school, sometimes with a friend on the back.

Chapter Two

What was Storthes Hall?

Rising demand for places had led to a fourth West Riding Asylum being built at Storthes Hall in 1904. That particular site was chosen as it not only balanced the distribution of hospitals across the county, but also allowed the actual buildings to be screened from neighbouring villages and communities by heavily wooded hillsides.

From the outset it was designed as a self-sufficient community. Its farm reared livestock for meat and milk and arable lands produced crops and vegetables. A poultry farm provided eggs and an additional source of meat and the orchards and gardens delivered apples, pears, plums, soft fruits and even flowers. The wider estate included extensive woodlands producing timber for maintenance and repairs and income from commercial sales. A bakery provided all the bread and pastries needed and the laundry catered for all the hygiene needs of a large institution. Uniforms for staff and clothing for patients were produced in the tailoring workshop. Footwear was made and repaired in the cobbler's shop and official documents were produced by the printing department. Engineering staff operated and maintained electric power and water supplies for the entire estate, prior to the introduction of the National Grid, together with heating for all the wards and offices. Although qualified professional staff managed each of the support functions, a significant proportion of the labour was provided by patients for both therapeutic and economic reasons. The original design also incorporated comprehensive sporting, recreational and social facilities for both patients and staff. A committee of the County Council managed the Asylum from its opening until the creation of the National Health Service in 1948.

Growing up in Storthes Hall Lane

As a child I was brought up to describe Storthes Hall as a hospital and to regard Asylum as a pejorative term; asylums housed inmates whereas hospitals treated patients. I could not understand why people suffering from a mental illness were regarded differently from patients with a physical complaint. We children living on the hospital estate treated its facilities and grounds as if they belonged to us. All our parents worked at the hospital in one capacity or another and we played in its buildings, gardens, fields and woodlands without let or hindrance. We even got to know many of the patients by name through attending their social facilities, such as the cinema shows on Wednesday evenings and theatrical performances by local amateur dramatic and operatic companies on Sunday evenings. As we grew older we used other social facilities, including the sports grounds for cricket, football and tennis, plus the indoor courts for badminton. As a teenager I played both soccer and cricket for hospital teams. The main administrative centre contained a superb hall with full size cinema screen and projection facilities and an enormous stage with state of the art lighting and effects and proper dressing rooms for theatrical performances. The hall seated several hundred people for films, plays, concerts and dances. After the war, members of staff formed an amateur dramatic society in which Dad was involved as both an actor and producer. I became a member in my teens.

The communal back-yard areas and the lack of any physical barriers between the houses encouraged a real sense of community which lasted throughout my childhood and adolescence. It was enhanced by the distance from the hospital estate to the nearest village and shops and the bus service being limited to once an hour. We grew up in the open air in a rural setting, despite being able to see the winding shafts of local collieries and the chimneys of woollen mills where yarn was woven into premium quality worsted cloth.

With so little vehicular traffic in those days, we used the road itself as a play-ground. In summer we would draw wickets with chalk on one of the front gates to the houses and bowl from the opposite side of the road. Behind the bowler's end were the soft fruit gardens of the hospital and to hit the ball into them was classed as a six and out. The guilty batsman had to fetch the ball and bring back a handful of strawberries, raspberries or currants for us to share. In the winter we raced each other on sledges down the road which sloped steeply.

Some local tradesmen had vans from which they sold their goods on weekly rounds. One of the farmers brought milk each day in metal churns in the back of a horse drawn cart. Our mothers would take different sized jugs to the cart to be filled. In winter he had a wagon with runners for the snow instead of wheels. Most of the farmers still used horses for ploughing and drawing carts and I recall being fascinated by their skill at the annual ploughing competition in a field adjoining the Cocked Hat wood (so called because of its triangular shape). With so many horses still being used in daily life, there was a busy blacksmith's forge on Penistone Road just past the Three Owls public house.

The varied skills of the occupants of the staff houses were regularly used for the benefit of fellow residents. One of the nursing attendants cut hair and joiners, electricians, plumbers and cobblers did repairs. Our kitchen was widely used as a surgery where cuts, scrapes, sprains and minor ailments were treated. I remember Dad giving anti-tetanus injections, putting stitches in bad cuts and dressing wounds for me and my friends. Although I knew it saved us money by not having to pay the doctor, I was too young to appreciate the enormity of the change from his war-time experiences in a tented military hospital under fire on a Normandy beach or in a Burmese jungle. I cannot over emphasise the importance of Dad's influence on my life. He was my role model before I even knew what a role model was and I learned so much from watching how he conducted himself in a variety of different situations. A big man, he had a commanding presence and exuded an air of firm but gentle authority.

In the summer months we played in the woods and built dams across the stream which ran through the valley at the bottom of the path leading across the fields to Farnley Tyas. You could drink from the unpolluted stream and we learned to tickle trout, although it was rare to catch one big enough to take home to eat. Our parents sometimes joined us for picnics when we gathered wild fruits such as blackberries and bilberries for our mothers to make into pies or jam. We also helped local farmers with hay-making and potato picking, for which we were paid two shillings and sixpence (12.5p) per day plus a cooked lunch.

One of the highlights of the year was November 5th, Bonfire Night, preceded by Mischief Night on the 4th. Mischief invariably comprised of knocking on doors and then running away, although sometimes two adjacent door knobs would be tied together, preventing either from opening. From late October we scoured the woods for logs and branches (chubbing in local dialect) and one of the dads would cut down a tree to provide the centre pole for the bonfire which was built in a nearby field. For the night itself, our mums made parkin and treacle toffee and we roasted potatoes in the embers of the fire. We were warned of the danger of fireworks but were lucky to be able to afford a few bangers, jumping crackers, sparklers and rockets. There was no organised display, but we pooled our meagre resources and made the best of what we had.

To progress in his career Dad knew he would have to gain general nursing certification. In 1948 he reverted from staff nurse status to student, with the consequent reduction in salary, to study in Birmingham for his State Registered Nurse (SRN) qualification, leaving us at home. It was hard for Mum to make ends meet whilst he was away. She often went without food so that Dilys and I had something to eat. Dad managed to get the normal three-year course reduced to two because of his wartime nursing experience.

As a nine year old in 1948, my recollections of the introduction of the NHS stem mainly from overhearing conversations between my parents and our neighbours. None of the families in Storthes Hall Lane were well off and it was a great relief for everyone that they no longer had to worry about how to pay for a visit to the doctor or dentist or for a prescription from the chemist.

Music was an important part of our family life. The first instrument I remember at home was a harmonium, later replaced by a piano. Dad played them both and we would often sing together as a family in the evenings, particularly in winter. When I was about eight or nine, Dad decided it was time for me to learn how to play. He started me off, but then I went for lessons at the home of one of the nursing staff, James Marsden. He was a violinist with the Yorkshire Symphony Orchestra and, although he couldn't play the piano, his knowledge of musical theory was outstanding and I progressed well under his tutelage. Most of the other families in the lane also had pianos or harmoniums and, before the advent of television, we would often get together for musical evenings.

When I was about twelve or thirteen, Mum decided I should learn how to dance and sent me for ballroom dancing lessons in Huddersfield at the Norah Bray School of Dancing. Norah Bray and her partner, Frank Noble, were the British professional champions at the time. Dilys already went there for ballet and tap lessons. I didn't like the idea at first, but soon warmed to it and gained bronze, silver and gold medals at Old Time and Modern dancing. It stood me in good stead as an older teenager when I was one of the only boys who could be relied upon to dance without treading on a girl's feet or kicking her, so I never went short of partners at a Saturday night dance.

As teenagers we all wanted to learn the guitar and play in a Skiffle group like our hero, Lonnie Donegan. One of my friends managed to acquire an old guitar which we shared to practice on, first of all playing just four strings using ukelele chords and later learning proper six string chords from the Bert Weedon "Teach Yourself the Guitar" tutor book.

When I was fifteen I took a part-time job at week-ends and in school holidays delivering bread for the Huddersfield Co-operative Society. I had to cycle the seven miles into Huddersfield to the bakery, where I joined one of the vans to help the driver on his rounds. This meant that Mum didn't have to buy me any clothes at all from then on and I could afford to go to the cinema or to a dance with my friends on Saturday evenings without having to ask for money. As a sixteen year old I went with three friends on a cycling holiday staying at youth hostels and covering more than a thousand miles in just over two weeks.

Hospital Staff

The Medical Superintendent, his Deputy and the Senior Psychiatrist also lived on the estate in large multi-roomed detached properties provided for them. I grew up knowing their houses and families quite well as Mum worked for each of them in turn as a cleaner, taking me with her before I was old enough to go to school. From time to time Dilys and I were the grateful recipients of good quality clothes which their children had outgrown.

The hospital became something of a haven for refugees before, during and after the Second World War, many of Jewish origin who had escaped from the Nazis. I particularly remember Doctor Schweder who had a flat in the staff residence for senior medical personnel above the administration block. She was a psychiatrist of German-Jewish extraction from Bohemia who managed to flee to the UK following the 1938 Munich agreement which allowed Hitler to occupy her homeland. From an early age I visited her apartment and, as I grew old enough to understand, she would talk to me about her home and how Prime Ministers Chamberlain and Daladier had betrayed Czechoslovakian democracy. She was a socialist and Zionist and made frequent visits to Israel after its creation as an independent state in 1948, bringing back mementos and photographs I can still picture on display in her flat. When I got to grammar school she would help me with my German homework if I was having particular difficulties, correcting my accent and encouraging me to read more widely. She enthralled me with the adventures of the 'Good Soldier Sweyk' and from an early age gave me books as presents. I remember ploughing through Dostoevsky's 'Crime and Punishment' at the age of about eleven. I think she saw in Dilys and me some of the family she had lost in the holocaust. Only after her death did I discover that the reason she felt especially close to me was that Dad had called her out to attend Mum for my birth because the local GP was busy with another patient.

From the age of sixteen, I worked as a porter at the hospital during school holidays and got to know many more people of European extraction; porters, cleaners, cooks, nursing and medical staff. I remember one of them particularly well. His birth name was Eduard Rosenfels, anglicised to Edward Redcliffe when he joined the British army. Born to Jewish communist parents in Vienna and raised as a dedicated party member, he was educated in Moscow through the '*Comintern*,' the international organisation formed in 1919 and dedicated to the establishment of world communism. In the 1930s, as Secretary of the Taxi-drivers' Trade Union in Vienna, he only just managed to escape the Gestapo following the '*Anschluss*,' the Nazi incorporation of Austria into the greater German Reich. He eventually made his way through the Balkans to Egypt and from there to England where he enlisted in the British army, ending the war as a sergeant interpreter in the British

Sector of occupied Germany. When the occupation ended, he refused an offer to go back to Austria to take a safe seat as an MP for the Communist Party. He became a naturalised British subject and lived the remainder of his life in Highburton, having married a local woman. An active Communist Party of Great Britain member until 1956, he left the party in protest against the suppression of the Hungarian revolution, but remained a left wing socialist. At lunch and tea breaks in the porters' room he would give me his copy of the Daily Worker (the British Communist Party newspaper) to read and get me to translate parts of it into German. Having learned most of his English in the army, he used me to help him improve his formal, rather than colloquial, English. He would tease me that Doctor Schweder had me speaking German like a Bohemian and that his own Viennese accent was far preferable. He was an intelligent man with an extensive knowledge and library of books on politics and philosophy in both English and German which he shared with me. An avid reader of local newspapers he was a frequent contributor to their letters pages.

Another of the porters was French. Georges Reynard had fled France after the German invasion to become a member of the Free French under General de Gaulle but left to work for the BBC's wartime service to occupied France. He then chose to remain in England instead of returning home after the allied victory. He too had lost most of his family during the war, but was reluctant to talk about them. We would speak French when working together and discussed life in France before and during the war. He was another very intelligent man who had chosen to hide himself within the hospital community, occasionally taking time off to go to London to participate in broadcasts on the BBC French service.

Others with whom I worked or got to know were from Poland, Estonia, Latvia and Greece, several, but not all, from Jewish backgrounds, each a victim of the Nazi occupations of their countries. Although differing widely in their political views and social origins, a common theme bound them together; hatred of fascism and a determination that it must never again be permitted to raise its ugly head in Europe. Through their tales of homes far away I began to learn and understand much more about life in the different countries of Europe. I am sure it was this that prevented me from regarding the English Channel as the barrier which protects Great Britain from continental encroachment which it became, and sadly still remains, for many of my generation.

In retrospect I have often wondered whether such an early exposure to other cultures and ideas propelled me into choosing to study languages and history at Grammar School rather than the sciences. Without doubt, however, those early experiences made a marked impression upon me, stimulating an interest in politics, history, literature and European affairs that I never lost. It was only many years later that I came to realise how unusual it was at that point in our history for a working class child growing up in a small Yorkshire community to be exposed to such a broad spectrum of European languages, politics, culture and thought.

Chapter Three

Infant & Junior School

I started school in September 1943 at the age of four and a half. Each day and in all weathers I walked with my friends the three miles by road (two across the fields) to Farnley Tyas Church of England Infant and Junior school. There was no school bus or scheduled service which would get us there for 9 a.m. and none of our parents had a car. The school had sixty pupils and three teachers, one in charge of about twenty children in each of the three classrooms. Miss Farrand taught reception and infants, Mrs Inman standards I & II and the headmistress, Mrs Wainwright, standards III, IV & V. The same three teachers remained in post for the whole of my time there. Hot meals in containers were delivered by van and were served from the school kitchen, supplemented by fresh vegetables from the school garden. I don't remember anyone going home for dinner. We helped to move desks and erect tables in the classroom where we ate our meal. The older children would then help to clear away cutlery and crockery and take them into the scullery to be washed by the solitary dinner lady, Mrs Thornton. A significant number of my fellow pupils received free school meals. Each of us also had one third of a pint of milk each day, a free health provision which carried on through secondary education until it was eventually removed in the 1970s by Margaret Thatcher as Secretary of State for Education.

I do remember being bitterly cold in winter, especially at school. The luckiest children were those whose desks were near the radiators, although the pipes themselves were often covered with items of clothing drying out. I can still recall the odour of warm, wet wool. All the boys wore short trousers so chapped knees were common. The school had two playgrounds separated by a high wall. Unusually for the time, the separation was by age and not gender, with infants together in one and juniors in the other. Outside lavatories for pupils were at the bottom of the playgrounds, the sole indoor toilet being reserved for our teachers. The cloak-rooms had wash hand basins with roller towels alongside and sufficient pegs and hooks for everyone's coats and hats.

The school was directly opposite the church. The Vicar would come into school two or three times a week to take assembly and teach us our catechism. The education I received was first class, helped by the fact that Mum had taught me to read before I commenced formal schooling. That early love of reading has stayed with me the whole of my life. Great emphasis was placed on literacy and numeracy, but good teachers imbued most of us with a desire to learn and improve ourselves. The school had a deservedly excellent academic reputation.

Discipline, although strict, was always fairly administered.

Most of the pupils came from working class families, the majority from the agricultural sector, children of both tenant farmers and farm labourers. Because of the school's excellent academic reputation, some middle class families from neighbouring villages took their children out of private education for their final year and sent them to Farnley to prepare them for the Scholarship (eleven plus) examination. Two such girls, who arrived in my final year, stood out from the rest of us by continuing to wear the uniforms of their former private schools.

I left in the summer of 1950, having passed the Scholarship examination and, courtesy of the 1944 Education Act, was awarded a free place to Royds Hall Grammar School (RHGS), a school supported jointly by Huddersfield County Borough and the West Riding Education Authorities. The standard and content of my elementary education had been so comprehensive that, in my first year at grammar school, the only new subjects I encountered were French, algebra and science. I had already covered the entire arithmetic and English language syllabus at junior school which had also provided me with an excellent grounding in poetry and literature.

Royds Hall Grammar School

RHGS was situated in Paddock, a suburb north-west of Huddersfield town centre. This meant I had to leave home at 7.30 a.m. and walk just over a mile to the main road to catch a bus into Huddersfield centre, where I took a trolley bus to Paddock, arriving at about 8.45 a.m. ready for lessons at 9 a.m. The school day ended at 4 p.m. and the return journey got me home between 5.30 and 6 p.m. In my later teens, weather permitting, I travelled to and from school by bicycle.

I had never visited RHGS before my first day and no-one else from Farnley Tyas had been awarded a place there, so I didn't know any of its 720 pupils. Such a large school was quite a change for someone from a junior school of just sixty children. Uniform was compulsory, its wearing was strictly enforced and the various items could only be purchased from two authorised retailers in Huddersfield. With Dad being away in Birmingham on student nurse pay, Mum applied for and received a grant from the West Riding Education Authority to assist with the purchase of my first uniform. I also received a free bus pass for the return journey to Huddersfield because of the distance I had to travel.

RHGS had a rigidly streamed four form entry. One or two pupils moved up or down after the first term and again at the end of the first year, but there was little change thereafter. The few children who entered aged thirteen on transfer from secondary modern schools were commonly referred to by both staff and pupils as 'late developers.' On arrival we assembled in the hall where names were called out and classes allocated. I was placed in the top stream and remained there throughout my time at RHGS. Homework was compulsory with a set timetable of three subjects per night Monday to Thursday and four at the weekend. I enjoyed my time at Grammar School and generally performed well, although not always to the standard expected by my teachers. Each month they prepared a formal report, grading us for attainment and effort in every subject. The highest grades attracted house points and the lowest extra work or even a Saturday morning detention. Twice yearly, at Christmas and mid-summer, we had examinations and at the end of each academic year a full report was completed which had to be countersigned by one of our parents. I still have that report book. Although they always encouraged me, neither of my parents was able to help me at all with homework or schoolwork.

Because we lived so far from the school, I was never able to mix with fellow pupils outside school hours until my late teens. It was also difficult to join in after school activities. However, I sang in the choir and in the fourth, fifth and sixth forms shared the piano playing in the newly formed school dance band. In my third year we had a new Physical Education teacher, a Yorkshire county sprinter on the fringe of international selection, who encouraged me to develop an interest in athletics. Under his coaching I became school champion in the hundred and two-twenty yards sprints, plus the high and long jump from the fourth form onwards and then inter-schools champion at the same events in my final year. I represented West Riding schools at the Northern Counties finals in 1957 at hundred yards, two-twenty yards, high jump and long jump. I also played tennis for the school from the fifth form onwards.

By 1955, the General Certificate of Education had replaced the former School Certificate examinations. We were restricted to a maximum of seven subjects at any one sitting at 'O' level, although that was later amended to eight when General Studies was introduced. All students were expected to sit a range of disciplines including languages, humanities and science. University entrance still required at least one 'O' level pass in a foreign language. Three subjects plus General Studies was considered sufficient at 'A' level. Exams themselves were not seen as particularly stressful as we had been constantly tested throughout our entire elementary and secondary education. I don't remember ever using or even hearing the word stress in connection with exams. In 1955 I gained eight 'O' levels in Mathematics, English Language, English Literature, French, German, Latin, History and General Studies and four 'A' levels in 1957 in French, German, History and General Studies. In the Sixth form I was appointed as a prefect and it was generally assumed that I would read modern languages at university prior to becoming a languages teacher.

In the fourth year our French and German teachers arranged pen friends for us to aid our written language skills. Somehow I ended up with a French girl as my pen friend instead of a boy and became the envy of all my friends over this mix-up. Janine lived in Lyon and her parents were teachers. We corresponded for a couple of years and then in 1956 she came to England and stayed at our house for two weeks. The following year, in July 1957, after my 'A' level exams, I went to stay with her family in Lyon.

I had not been abroad before so had to apply for a passport and had also never been away on my own, let alone to a foreign country. Dad booked my tickets through Thomas Cook's in Huddersfield and details of my itinerary and arrival time were sent by post to Janine's parents. I travelled by train to London, then on to Newhaven for the boat-train to Paris where I had to change stations for the final leg of the journey to Lyon. All of this was not only exciting but quite scary. I eventually made it to Lyon, but had somehow mixed up the twenty-four hour clock and instead of arriving at 3pm I got there at 3am, so spent the rest of the night in the station waiting room. I managed to catch a bus to Janine's home and quite surprised her mother by ringing the front door bell at 7am. At the end of my two weeks stay, Janine's family were going on holiday and her father asked me if I would like to come with them. Naturally I said yes and so off we all went in their car to a gite in the village of Le Chambon sur Lignon in the Massif Central. I completely forgot to let my parents know until we had been there for a couple of days. We didn't have a phone at home and neither did any of our neighbours, so I had to send a postcard, which arrived about a week later and belatedly put my parents' minds at rest. It took a little longer for them to come to terms with my thoughtlessness.

Janine's family was much better off financially than mine and her parents were very generous to me. We visited so many places that I felt I was really getting to know France. My spoken French improved enormously with having to use it all the time. I was astonished to find that neither of her parents, both teachers, spoke a single word of English. Eventually I had to return home and they helped me re-arrange train times so that I would arrive in Huddersfield at a reasonable hour. I arrived back just in time for the family holiday in Whitby.

Chapter Four

Mum and Dad were both brought up in the Salvation Army (SA). They met and fell in love whilst serving as officer cadets at the SA Training College, Denmark Hill in London. On completion of their training the SA posted Dad to the Lake District and Mum to Sussex. For almost three years the SA hierarchy refused them permission to marry, so they reluctantly resigned their commissions. Dad then chose to pursue a career in nursing. They never wavered in their faith, however, and finally joined the Methodist Church in which they both became lay preachers. Dilys and I were raised to be practical Christians, a faith in which helping others in need took precedence over professed belief or doctrinal conformity.

Highburton Methodist Chapel

Most of my Sunday school and teenage church attendance was at Highburton, a former Primitive Methodist Chapel. Because of the limited bus service on Sundays, adult worship was held at 2.30 p.m. and 6 p.m. with Sunday school at 10.30 a.m. With so many chapels in the mainly rural circuit, the pulpit was more often than not occupied by a lay preacher. As the minister only visited us four times a year, some of the lay preachers were authorised to preside at Holy Communion services.

As a child I attended morning Sunday school and afternoon worship, to which the evening service was added as I grew older. The chapel was the hub of social and community activities for Highburton, there being no other place of worship of any denomination in the village. Throughout the 1940s, 1950s and early 1960s it was extremely well attended. Shops other than newsagents were closed and Sunday cinema attendance was frowned upon.

Our Sunday School Superintendent was Mr. Oldroyd, who was also a lay preacher. He reminded me of one of the Biblical patriarchs with his silver hair and aura of authority. He was strict but we loved him and he was a wonderful story teller. We had both male and female Sunday school teachers who worked hard to guide us through the Bible and Methodist history. Each year a Scripture Examination Competition was organized by the Circuit with the Sunday school gaining the highest marks being presented with a silver Rose Bowl trophy. We were regular winners, so good was our grounding and preparation.

Chapel and Sunday School Anniversaries were very special occasions. Mrs Gertie Stringer was our organist and choir mistress. She chose the hymns and anthems for the annual services and drilled both the children's and adult choirs until they were note and word perfect. She taught us to sing in harmony and how to read our parts from music. Special preachers would be invited to lead these services which ensured a large congregation and full pews.

The annual Sunday school outings were always popular and ranged from walks in the local countryside with games and a picnic to coach trips to the seaside. Concerts and social events of all kinds attracted good attendances from the village, particularly among those who didn't come to Sunday services. The two highlights were the annual pantomime, which Dad produced in the 1950s and 1960s, and the Sale of Work each autumn, for which Mum worked tirelessly. Coupons for the latter were sold throughout the year which could then be redeemed on the day. In a poor working class community recovering from the hardships of the war years, this was a great boon as a means of acquiring household goods people couldn't afford to buy outright. Hire purchase and consumer credit had yet to arrive on the scene.

I was received into junior membership at thirteen and adult membership at sixteen. We had a strong youth fellowship for teenagers and our leaders organised visits to Cliff College in Derbyshire for the Whitsuntide Weekend Rally and then for a full week to the Derwent Convention in summer. As most of us came from families with no money to spare we were able to reduce the cost by going as volunteers, helping with meal preparation, serving, clearing away and washing up. We also went hiking with our leaders, often taking the train into Lancashire and then walking back over the Pennines via one of the old pack-horse trails. As older teenagers a group of us went on holiday together to Bridlington staying at a Christian guest house.

All the churches in the area played an important role in the life of the village. Walks of public witness were held each year at Whitsuntide, parading through the streets with banners and led by brass bands. In Kirkburton the walks terminated on the cricket ground off Riley Lane, where stalls were set up, teas were served and choirs from all the different denominations joined together for 'The Sing', usually a rendering of Handel's 'Messiah' or a similar work, to the accompaniment of the Salvation Army band and a local brass band.

At 11.30pm on Christmas Eve, members from the chapel would gather at our house and then walk through Highburton and Kirkburton villages, stopping at pre-arranged locations to sing carols. They would be out almost all night and received refreshment at various houses en-route whose owners had prepared tea, mince pies and Christmas cake in advance. I couldn't wait to be old enough to join them for the first time. It was a great occasion and local people would deliberately stay up into the early hours just to hear us.

During the war years, the Salvation Army Hall in Kirkburton was widely used by troops stationed in the village and surrounding area as a social centre at which tea and refreshments were served. Local people would gather to offer hospitality and Aunty Gwyneth met Emlyn, her future husband, there. After the war Mum and Dad would often go there to meet friends and the whole family would attend Sunday Meetings whenever relatives who were Salvationists visited us. In his retirement Dad led the Silver Threads group for older people.

My personal theology has developed and expanded throughout my life and is central to who and what I am. Those early roots, nourished and tended by my parents and Sunday school teachers, have become deeply established. They have been a constant presence in my life as our family has moved around the country. The church has always been our primary reference point on arriving in a new town. My growing understanding of the implications of the teachings of Jesus has shaped my political allegiance and has also provided the moral and ethical grounds for making a choice when facing difficult professional decisions.

Chapter Five

National Service

Conscription into the armed forces for all men between eighteen and forty-one years of age, not employed in reserved occupations, was announced by the government in September, 1939. After the end of the Second World War conscription was retained and men between the ages of eighteen and twenty-one were required to serve for two years in one of the three armed services. Deferments in order to complete an apprenticeship or undergraduate degree were permissible. Complete exemption was only granted on medical grounds or for reasons of conscience. The last National Service conscripts were demobilised in 1963.

I entered the Royal Air Force in 1958 on my nineteenth birthday, reporting to the RAF reception centre at Cardington in Bedfordshire where we were medically examined, had our hair cut and were issued with uniforms and basic equipment. Our civilian clothing was sent home as we were not permitted to wear anything other than uniform for the duration of our initial training.

At Cardington both national servicemen and regular entrants were interviewed and assessed to determine which area of work in the RAF they were most suited for. I appeared before an officer selection board which, after a series of tests, provisionally accepted me for a short service commission as an interpreter. This would require me to sign on for a nine year engagement, the first three of which would be spent at Cambridge University reading for a degree in Russian. Attending university on a Pilot Officer's salary rather than a student grant with fees paid by the Ministry of Defence quite appealed to me.

Initial Training at RAF Wilmslow

I then travelled to RAF Wilmslow in Cheshire to undergo the three months basic training programme common to all entrants known as 'Square Bashing.' My entire intake consisted of national servicemen from a variety of social backgrounds and geographical locations. We were billeted in corrugated iron Nissen huts, each accommodating about twenty beds, which were freezing cold in winter and boiling hot in summer. The only heating was a cast iron pot-bellied stove in the middle of the billet. We were each allocated an iron framed single bed, a tall wooden locker in which to hang our uniforms and a bedside locker for storing smaller items. Everyone had his own 'bed-space' to keep tidy and clean. Leading from the hut was a corridor to the ablutions block where the washing and toilet facilities were located.

The corporal in charge of our squad slept in a separate room at one end of the hut. We soon learned that, according to the RAF, this man was the most important person in our lives. It almost felt as if he had the power of life or death over us. His job was to turn us into the top squad by the end of our training which, in turn, reflected on his ability as an instructor. He had to teach us how to care for our uniforms and equipment, how to develop discipline and team spirit through drill and handle personal weaponry, such as the Lee Enfield .303 rifle and generally how to do everything the RAF way.

The billet was filthy when we entered and we had to transform it into a pristine state in as short a time as possible. Floors had to be waxed and polished to a high gloss, windows had to sparkle and every bed had to be laid out in prescribed military fashion with sheets and blankets folded into a bed-pack and kit laid out on the mattress for inspection. Our uniforms had to be pressed by hand, buttons and brassware polished and toe-caps of boots 'bulled' to resemble patent leather. Several of my squad had never been away from home before and had never even had to clean their own shoes or make their own bed, so service life came as quite a shock. Some of them sobbed themselves to sleep at night. Daily checks by our corporal and weekly inspections by an officer wearing white gloves reinforced the importance of getting everything just right.

On top of all this we had to learn to march as a unit and perform manoeuvres by command, learn how to assemble and disassemble a rifle, attach a bayonet and hit a target on the firing range. We marched everywhere as a squad. Discipline was strict, we had to obey orders instantaneously and without question or summary punishment known as fatigues would follow as sure as night follows day. This ranged from performing meaningless tasks such as cutting the grass with a pair of nail scissors or moving things from one place to another and then putting them back. The aim was to stop us behaving as individuals and make us think and act as a unit, looking to a leader for direction. Individual initiative was actively discouraged and punishments were imposed on the entire unit for the errors of one person so that peer-group pressure would bring the offender into line. We soon learned that the only real offence was to be caught. By and large the system worked in that we accepted the necessity to conform if only to avoid extra fatigues. In the communal environment of the billet we had to learn how live with each other on reasonably amicable terms, which took some much longer than others to get used to.

As training progressed, arrangements for future duties were firmed up and various trade designations were made following further interviews. I was still programmed to become an interpreter. Remarkably my unit became quite proficient at drill and managed to reach adequate standards with both the rifle and light machine gun, except for one idiot who nearly mowed down half the squad by trying to fire a bren-gun left handed. The worst part was entering and remaining for a set time in a chamber filled with tear gas without a respirator. Quite a number were physically sick afterwards. We then had to do it again, but this time wearing a gas mask to give us confidence in its use.

Our corporal came into the billet one lunch time and instructed everyone over five feet eight inches in height and who did not wear glasses to fall in on the square. We presumed this meant another drill parade for some ceremony or other but were astonished to be addressed by a Warrant Officer (WO) who thanked us all for volunteering to re-muster to the RAF Police. We were stunned into silence as everyone had already been allocated or had chosen a trade classification. Bravely, or foolishly, I stepped forward and stated that, with regret, I could not comply as I was going to be an officer and an interpreter. The WO's brusque and loosely translated riposte was that officers are useless appendages. Senior NCO's make all the important decisions and I was going into the guardroom either as a member of the RAF police or under close arrest for disobeying a lawful order. It was for me to choose. I stepped back and accepted my fate, little realising the impact on my future life.

My squad didn't manage to win the drill prize, much to the chagrin of our corporal who had pushed us hard over the final days. Our final task, after being informed of our postings, was to dirty our immaculate billet in preparation for the next intake of recruits. That was the RAF way.

Police Training at RAF Netheravon

My next posting was to the RAF Police Training School at Netheravon on Salisbury Plain in Wiltshire. There I spent eight weeks studying criminal law, Queen's Regulations, Air Council Instructions and the powers, duties and responsibilities of the RAF Police. Off duty we were allowed to leave camp and would walk to the local village, a beautiful little place with thatched cottages and a river in which we could swim. The down side was an open sewer running along the main street.

One day during training we were asked if anyone had any proficiency in foreign languages. I replied that I had French and German at 'A' level and good conversational ability in both. The education officer tested me and was highly delighted. He then told me I was to be posted to NATO HQ, Fontainebleau just south of Paris, where all staff had to be conversant in more than one language. I would need to be measured for a specially tailored uniform as this was a prestige posting. It seemed too good to be true at the time he said it, a completely unexpected compensation for my earlier disappointment at not becoming an interpreter. I was duly measured for my new uniform and went to evening classes to brush up my languages but then the blow fell. The Americans invaded Lebanon and all overseas postings for national servicemen were cancelled, so I never got my tailored uniforms and, instead of Paris and NATO HQ, I was posted to RAF Manby in Lincolnshire.

RAF Manby

RAF Manby housed a flying training college, a NATO guided weapons school, an RAF Group HQ and an operational flying station. It housed around two thousand staff with an Air Vice-Marshall and an Air

Commodore in permanent residence. It also incorporated a satellite airfield a few miles away at Strubby, which was retained for operational use because of its long runways.

The twenty-two strong RAF police section was commanded by Sergeant Dick Sheppard, a long serving NCO who drank like a fish and was inordinately proud of his ginger waxed moustache. Three regular corporals completed the command team. The seventeen policemen already in post when I arrived were all national servicemen, the majority with good educational backgrounds. At six months service I was promoted to leading aircraftman (LAC) and six months later to senior aircraftman (SAC) although for the latter I first had to pass an examination. A month after reaching SAC I was promoted to Corporal, at which level I spent the remainder of my two years' military service.

The guardroom had to be manned and patrols carried out for the full twenty-four hours so we convinced Sgt Sheppard to let us design our own shift system. We chose to work for nine consecutive days and then have four days off, which gave us a better chance of getting home during the break. The pattern selected was three night shifts (2359 to 0900) three evenings (1700 to 2359) and three days on (0900 to 1700) followed by three days off starting back at 2359 on the fourth. We would often work a combined day and evening shift to get extra free time.

Police work tended to be routine and often boring. Physical security had to be maintained by vehicle checks and regular patrols, especially when the threat level by the IRA was deemed to be high. Discipline on the camp had to be upheld, dress codes adhered to and minor infringements dealt with. I cannot remember a single case of desertion, but absence without leave was common. Occasionally real crime would provide more interest. Personal assaults were usually the product of too much alcohol and, although theft from comrades was universally deplored, theft from the RAF itself was almost expected, if not actually condoned. Stores of all kinds would disappear, but the most common theft was that of petrol. Aircraft returning from abroad were also used to smuggle in cigarettes and alcohol which would be dropped over the outskirts of the airfield on small parachutes prior to landing so that the aircraft could be formally searched on its arrival by HM Customs & Excise and RAF police without anything illegal being there to be found.

Although we had to practice regularly on the firing range to maintain competence with the .38 Smith and Wesson service revolver, the only time we were actually required to carry a loaded weapon was when acting as escort to the finance officer during his weekly visit to the bank in Louth to collect money for pay parades.

Life on Camp
Sport was encouraged in the RAF and I played tennis, soccer and basketball for RAF Manby and represented Flying Training Command at basketball. We held our own against other British teams, but were regularly slaughtered by United States Air Force teams based in Lincolnshire and East Anglia.

Just across from the main entrance to the camp was a very small Methodist Chapel where evening worship was held each Sunday. One of the attractions of going there was that members of a local farming family from the nearby village of Grimoldby would attend the Sunday evening service. If Harold or Muriel West could not be present personally, then one of their three unmarried daughters would invite any RAF personnel at the service back to the farm for supper, a walk of about three miles each way, but well worth the effort. I looked forward to those evenings immensely and spent many happy hours playing the piano for hymn singing in their front room and enjoying the conversation and food around the dining table.

There was also a small nonconformist chapel on the camp itself and a local Methodist minister acted as the Other Denominations (OD) chaplain. Only Anglicans were required to attend compulsory church parades. Jews, Catholics and Other Denominations were ordered to fall out from the parade. We ODs used to meet on Thursday evenings for a short service and I usually played the harmonium. The chapel also had a small quiet room that could be used instead of going to the NAAFI.

In many ways life in the RAF was like living in a cocoon. We all had a job and everything was provided, from food and accommodation to clothing, laundry and comprehensive medical and dental services. Weekly pay was meagre, at least for national servicemen, but all it had to cover was spending money. Off duty activities were provided through the NAAFI and Corporals' Club, the Astra cinema, the lending library, evening classes and the radio network. Educational, sporting and social events were organised on a regular basis and it was quite possible to serve the whole of one's engagement without going off camp except for annual leave. Manby Forces Network (MFN) radio station broadcast programmes for four hours each evening, mainly music, local news and interviews and I became one of its presenters. We were given a generous allowance to buy the latest records and the content of broadcasts was not censored. Copying the popular BBC radio programme "Brain of Britain", a "Brain of Manby" competition was organised annually by the education officer. I won it in 1959, following the success of a colleague the previous year, much to the delight of Sergeant Sheppard who took credit for all the achievements of his national service policemen.

The nearest town of any size to camp was Louth, a short bus journey away. The busy little market town had a surfeit of Public Houses, open all hours on market days. More important to me was the dance each Saturday evening in the Town Hall with music provided by a small live band, 'Cyril and his Music.' Shifts permitting I went to the dance.

I managed to meet a member of the WRAF, Kathleen Rumsey, who worked in Air Traffic Control. I had already seen her at Manby chapel and the Saturday dance in Louth. I was attracted to her and plucked up courage to ask her to go to one of the dances with me. She accepted and that was the start our life together, although neither of us knew it at the time.

Getting home as often as possible was the aim of most national servicemen and the best and cheapest way so to do was to hitch hike. Provided you were in uniform there was never a problem attracting a lift as almost every family had experience of a relative in the forces who wanted to get home.

Life developed into a routine, broken occasionally by duty at Strubby as the solitary RAF police presence, working 8 a.m. to midnight in the guardroom and then sleeping there in a small room at the back. I believed I was performing my duties satisfactorily, but vividly remember Sgt Sheppard crudely telling me, "You will never make a policeman as long as you have a hole in your arse." I reminded him of that comment some thirty years later after my appointment as Chief Constable of Humberside when I visited him at his home in retirement near Grimsby.

His response was typical. Despite my failings, he asserted, some of his training and advice must have sunk in.

My relationship with Kathleen developed and deepened. We went out together on and off-camp as often as we could and visited our respective homes during leave. I don't actually remember when it was that I knew I was in love with her, but as my demobilisation date drew nearer I realised I couldn't just leave and never see her again. I do remember standing outside the WRAF block one evening and asking her if we could get engaged when I was demobbed. She agreed and we celebrated my demob, engagement and twenty-first birthday at the Palace theatre-club in Huddersfield with Dilys and her (then) boyfriend. We bought each other engagement rings in Huddersfield. Although she tried to hide it, my Mum was not pleased that I had chosen to marry someone she didn't know well without having first sought either her advice or approval.

Following the end of my national service, Kathleen remained in the WRAF to complete her four-year engagement, whilst I had to sort out my future. I went back to Manby on several occasions to see her, staying at a house in the nearby village until she completed her service and moved to Sheffield and shared a flat with one of her former WRAF colleagues, Betty Borthwick.

Chapter Six

Teaching and Goldsmiths' College

Whilst in the RAF I applied to Goldsmiths' College, University of London, to read for a degree in modern languages and was offered a place at the beginning of the 1960/61 academic year. In the meantime I had to earn some money and applied to the West Riding Education Authority for a temporary teaching post. Following an interview with the Director of Education for the Huddersfield area, I was given a post at Colne Valley High School, a new comprehensive school of 1,500 pupils at Linthwaite. I started after the Easter break and after seeing the headmaster, was sent to the Marsden annexe, the former council school building in which Dad had been a pupil. I taught English and History to eleven to thirteen year olds. Fortunately this was still in the days of set text-books, so I was usually able to keep one or two lessons ahead of the class. I enjoyed my time at Colne Valley High School and related well with staff and pupils. I was able to renew acquaintance with a couple of my former teachers from Royds Hall, who had taken up senior posts at the new school.

In the school summer holidays I had to turn my mind to university in September and worked again at the hospital to earn some extra money. I received a full grant from the West Riding Education Authority plus a special allowance from the local parish council towards books.

I received notification from Goldsmiths' College that I had been allocated a place in one of its halls of residence, Loring Hall, near Foots Cray in Kent. Full costs of food and accommodation were covered by the local authority grant, but I had to buy a season ticket to cover the cost of rail travel to and from college at New Cross each day. Loring Hall was a former residence of Lord Canning, Prime Minister in the early nineteenth century and accommodated some thirty male students in two, three and four bedded rooms.

I'm not particularly proud of my time at Goldsmiths. At college I was active in the Campaign for Nuclear Disarmament (CND), Anti-Apartheid (AA) and MethSoc. On Sunday evenings I would travel up to the Kingsway Hall in central London to hear the Reverend Dr Donald Soper preach. I remember him explaining that being a socialist was how he put into practice his understanding of the essential message of Jesus, a statement that greatly influenced my own development. I immersed myself in student politics and was elected to the Students' Union. I played sport and joined the debating society where I was awarded half colours for representing Goldsmiths in inter-college debating competitions, but foolishly didn't study hard enough to make up the gap caused by National Service and consequently failed my Part I exams. I had, therefore, to leave after the end of my first year causing considerable disappointment to my parents who felt I had thrown away an excellent opportunity to better myself.

I went back to work at the hospital temporarily, but had to find a permanent job that would provide for Kathleen and me when we were married. She had by this time left the WRAF and was sharing a flat with Betty in Sheffield where they both worked as telephonists for the GPO.

Chapter Seven

Joining the Lancashire Constabulary

With the need for a permanent job in mind and remembering my National Service, I came across a Home Office advert in the paper for police recruits which listed forces with current vacancies. Dad put me in touch with a county councillor who lived locally and also someone from the Huddersfield Borough police. They were both very helpful and enabled me to make the decision to seek a career in the police service. Most importantly they explained the difference between the county and borough forces which existed at the time and what that meant in terms of balancing the opportunities for career progression against domestic stability. Following this meeting I decided to apply to the Lancashire Constabulary. Although I did tell Kathleen what I had done, I don't remember asking her whether or not she wanted to join me in embarking on this new venture. I suppose that in the absence of a clear "No," I simply assumed that she would come with me.

Again I disappointed my mother by choosing to move away from home. She made it clear that, in her opinion, a police constable did not have the social status of a graduate teacher and was not a good enough profession for her son. She maintained that position until I was promoted to Inspector when she pronounced that she had always known I would do well. Thank you Mum!

To join the Lancashire Constabulary, I had first to take a series of tests which I sat at Kirkburton police station. There the duty sergeant told me that Lancashire had the reputation of being the most progressive force in the country. It was also the largest outside London, so career prospects were good.

I was called for a series of interviews at Lancashire Constabulary HQ, Hutton, in November 1961. I was immediately accepted and was offered a place starting on 8th January 1962. My first two weeks were spent at the force training school at Stanley Grange near Preston where we were issued with uniforms and accoutrements, briefed about the organisation and structure of the Lancashire Constabulary and what it had to offer in career terms. Because it was so unusual for someone with 'A' levels to apply to become a police officer, I was constantly being asked "Why on earth do you want to join the police?" At that stage, I didn't have a satisfactory answer. After National Service, life at Stanley Grange was quite relaxed and I was able to use the library and museum to find out more about my new employer. When I was issued with collar number 1569 I was told that two previous holders had been sacked and another had committed suicide. "Maybe you will break the jinx" the sergeant observed. Once again I was lost for words.

The next thirteen weeks were spent at the No 1 District Home Office Police Training Centre Bruche, Padgate, near Warrington, which provided training for all forces in the north west of England. Padgate was a former RAF camp which had been used as a teacher training college immediately after the war to meet the desperate need for teachers in peace-time. Although some new buildings had been erected, much of the living accommodation was in war-time wooden huts similar to those in which I had undergone my RAF square-bashing.

Training consisted of formal lectures in criminal, traffic and general law, police practice and administrative procedures, plus practical exercises, role playing, first aid, fitness training, drill and life-saving. Weekly tests kept us focussed on our studies as a pass mark of seventy per cent was required. In order to graduate, we not only had to pass the final examination but also be able to swim eighteen consecutive lengths in the pool, gain the Royal Life Saving Society's Bronze Medallion and the St John Ambulance First Aid Certificate.

Much of the law had to be committed to memory and we were given a series of legal definitions to learn each week. I found the workload relatively easy to manage and quite enjoyed encountering new subjects. I was fascinated to learn that the police were founded as peace keepers rather than law enforcers. I expected to be told that we must be impartial but was surprised to hear that being non-political means voting Conservative. I had time for sport and represented the centre at football and tennis. The working week included Saturday mornings, so it was a rush to get home and back before midnight on Sunday. Some weekends I would travel to Sheffield to stay with Kathleen and Betty.

On conclusion of the Home Office course, we returned to Stanley Grange for a further two weeks to familiarise ourselves with the procedures and systems used by the Lancashire Constabulary. I used the library to research further into the history of the British police. The Assistant Chief Constable (Personnel) stated he was delighted with my performance at Bruche and Stanley Grange and informed me that I was to be posted to Atherton section of Leigh Division. I had never even heard of Atherton and as I didn't know where it was, had to look it up on a map.

Probation at Atherton

After a week's home leave, I made my way to my new posting and arrived in Market Street, Atherton, by bus from Manchester carrying two suitcases of clothes and uniforms with my helmet in a brown paper bag. On leaving the bus I had to ask a passer-by how to find the Police Station. I introduced myself at the front desk and was invited into the office to be welcomed by those on duty. Sergeant Wignall, who had previously served as an instructor at Bruche, greeted me with the words, "Welcome lad, what's the definition of a Part I firearm?" Fortunately I was able to answer word perfectly, whereupon he announced to all present that I had a bright future in the job. He then told one of the PCs to show me to my lodgings, instructing me to return in full uniform within the hour. Fortunately my new home was only a couple of hundred yards from the police station. My landlady was a widow with four adult sons, all older than me. She lived alone and had offered to provide lodgings for a policeman for company and security. I quickly warmed to her and she, in return, treated me almost as another son. I gradually got to know her family who were delighted that she no longer had to live alone.

The police station was a post-war two storey building with offices in the centre and living accommodation at either end. The ground floor contained the front office, cloakroom and a detention room which also doubled as the report writing room. Upstairs was a combined locker/dining room and kitchen, the CID office and lavatory. At the rear was the bicycle shed and kennels for stray dogs.

Atherton had a complement of three uniformed sergeants and fifteen constables. Combined with the adjacent town of Tyldesley, with a similar sized staff, it formed a sub-division commanded by Inspector Bartholomew, also known as Black Bart. I never found out whether this was because of his dubious character or his habit of using mascara to colour his greying moustache. One day he got caught in the rain and the mascara ran down either side of his mouth making him look like Charlie Chan, the fictional Chinese detective. A detective sergeant and a detective constable provided the CID cover for both towns. The two dog handlers based at Tyldesley were responsible for the eastern half of the division. A solitary unmarked radio equipped car, call sign S437, covered the two towns.

Both towns were Urban District Council areas, with their own town halls and elected councillors. Each had a population of around twenty thousand, the majority of whom were working class and lived on large council estates. Atherton UDC area contained three collieries, two cotton mills, a steel works, a nut and bolt factory, a manufacturing chemist plant, two large haulage companies plus numerous small light-engineering works. It was also the headquarters of the Lancashire United Transport bus company. Mining and engineering employees were almost entirely male, whereas the majority of workers in the cotton mills were female. Although there were Anglican, Methodist, Unitarian and Salvation Army buildings in the town, Roman Catholics seemed to be in the majority. The population was uniformly white, with no black or minority ethnic residents.

The towns were self-sufficient in terms of social and shopping facilities, nearly all the shops being locally owned. Chain stores or supermarkets had not yet arrived on the scene. Each town had a cinema and a variety of social and sporting clubs. It seemed as though there was a pub on every street corner, some of which were only licenced to sell beer.

We worked a forty-eight hour week in three basic shifts of 6 a.m. to 2 p.m., 2 p.m. to 10 p.m. and 10 p.m. to 6 a.m. with one day off per week and one weekend off in seven. The police station was manned between 9 a.m. and 1 a.m. by senior constables and outside those hours one of the beat patrols would call in at hourly intervals to receive any telephone messages from Divisional Headquarters (DHQ).

The town was divided into four beats, two on foot covering the town centre and two cycle beats covering the outlying areas. We had to provide our own cycles and were paid nine old pence per shift for each day's use. The force VHF radio network only covered motor vehicles, so the sole means of communication was via the network of public telephone kiosks. Before commencing a tour of duty, we would be given a schedule of times and locations at which we could be available for contact by the station duty constable. We had to arrive at a nominated kiosk five minutes prior to the appointed time and remain there for ten minutes. Outside that period we were completely out of touch with the station and our supervisors.

Probationer constables had to complete homework set by the force training department on a monthly basis. The work was marked by the divisional training officer and returned to the station for review by the sergeants and the inspector before being placed in our personal files. One day a month we had to attend DHQ for an oral test to make sure we had actually done the work ourselves. I consistently did well and was graded as the probationer with the best prospects in the division, which drew my name to the attention of both the divisional commander and his deputy.

Promotion examinations at that time consisted of two elements, professional and educational. Previous academic qualifications did not provide exemption from the educational element. That part of the examination could be taken during the probationary period, so I sat mine at the very first opportunity in November 1962, passing easily at the first attempt and qualifying straight through to the level needed for promotion to inspector. I was the only probationer constable in the entire force to do that in 1962.

A minimum of four years' service had to be completed before being allowed to sit the professional examination for qualification to sergeant, with a minimum of five years' service required to be eligible for actual promotion. In the early 1960s the average length of service as a constable, prior to promotion to sergeant, was between ten and fifteen years. Separate papers in criminal law, traffic law and regulations and general law plus administrative procedures had to be passed at one sitting. A local barrister confided that the standard of knowledge required was higher than that needed to qualify for the bar and without having recourse to legal textbooks. The professional examination to inspector could not be taken until the rank of sergeant had been achieved. I remember thinking how good it would be to reach the rank of Inspector.

The Lancashire Constabulary took its training responsibilities very seriously, requiring probationers to serve in all the main branches of policing to gain an insight into their functions and to assess potential for future specialisation. Most of this occurred during the second year of probation after having received a good grounding on foot patrol.

In retrospect, Atherton was an ideal place to begin my new career. It was small enough to allow me to get to know a good proportion of the population, yet large enough to provide experience across a wide range of policing activities. Most crime was property based, such as theft and breaking into houses or shops. Violence, however, was invariably linked with drunkenness, domestic assault or both. A high level of alcohol related disorder would be encountered at week-ends and following pay day at the local collieries. We usually patrolled the town centre in pairs rather than singly on Friday and Saturday evenings.

Although traffic infringements provided the main source of legal process, we were encouraged and expected to be competent in dealing with all aspects of maintaining the peace. The Inspector prosecuted cases in the local Magistrates' Court and probationer constables had to give oral evidence in all their cases, including guilty pleas, as part of their training.

The policy of renting council houses for police officers within the heart of the community being policed was extremely successful. It allowed for no separation or division between the police and the population being policed. We lived next door to each other and encountered each other both on and off duty. We shopped in the same street and socialised in the same places. Our children went to the same schools and so on. Police pay at that time also placed us on the same financial level as the average industrial worker, although lower than that of coal miners. Robert Peel, founder of the English police, would have been pleased to know that his original principles were still being applied.

At the end of the first year, probationers returned to Bruche for a two-week residential course to assess progress and cover certain aspects of criminal law more deeply. I came top in the exam at the end of the course.

In the second year we served various attachments to different departments, two weeks at DHQ to learn how the administration operated, four weeks in the traffic branch and eight weeks with the CID. I enjoyed all of these, but was particularly successful on the CID attachment, making a number of arrests and working well with the local Detective Sergeant (DS) who spent considerable time showing me how to put together a crime file for prosecution. He stressed that all the work that went into the detection of a crime and arrest of an offender would be completely wasted if the relevant court file turned out to be evidentially deficient or otherwise inadequate to secure a conviction. In return I helped him to prepare for the traffic paper for his inspector's exam which he had already failed twice.

The entire division only had two full-time Scenes of Crime Officers (SOCO), so we were expected to do elementary crime scene examinations ourselves, only sending for a SOCO when it was clear there was important evidence to be obtained. We also took our own elimination fingerprints and those of persons in custody. Dealing with sudden deaths and attending post-mortems was a regular feature of uniformed activity. I dealt with five such deaths during my first month at Atherton. The pathologist was a fascinating man, an Austrian Jewish refugee from the Nazis. Each PC reporting a death had to take notes for him at the PM and he told me I was the only one who didn't seem to have problems with his accent. I shared with him the story of my friend Edward, the porter at Storthes Hall hospital. We would exchange a few words in German which he appreciated as none of his medical colleagues at Wigan Infirmary spoke the language. "Polizist Anton, du sprichst wie echte Wiener" (Policeman Anthony, you speak like a genuine Viennese) he told me. It wasn't true, but he was that sort of man. I really liked him. He was researching industrial diseases of the lungs such as pneumoconiosis and asbestosis, but ironically was a chain smoker who invariably smoked during a PM with ash often dropping from his cigarette on to the body being examined.

At the end of the second year we returned to Bruche for a final two-week course and examination. Once again I came top and, following an interview with the Assistant Chief Constable (Personnel) at force headquarters, my appointment as a constable in the Lancashire Constabulary was confirmed. The icing on the cake was the pay rise that went along with the successful completion of my probationary period. During my time at Atherton I regularly played football for the divisional team and represented the force at athletics.

Chapter Eight

Marriage and a new Family

Kathleen and I were married at Hope Methodist Chapel in Derbyshire on 8 September 1962 and honeymooned in York. On our return we went into lodgings with a widow in Stanley Street, Atherton, as there were no police owned or rented houses available. We had a bedroom to ourselves but shared her kitchen for cooking and eating. In November 1962, one of the married constables was transferred to another division for disciplinary reasons. He had left his house in such a disgusting state that no-one wanted to move in, so in January 1963 it was offered to us. We didn't really have a choice as it was made clear that if we refused we would go to the bottom of the list.

Not only was the house dirty and in need of complete internal redecoration, but the PC had neglected to drain the cistern and turn off the water before he left. During the sub-zero temperatures of December 1962 and January 1963 every-thing had frozen solid, including the back boiler behind the fireplace. As this was the only source of heating and hot water, we were unable to light a fire and had to keep warm and thaw the twenty-one burst pipes throughout the house using paraffin heaters and electric fires borrowed from colleagues. Because of the poor internal state of the house, the Police Authority agreed to pay for the cost of redecoration outside the normal schedule.

The house at 5, Maple Avenue, was one of a number of council houses on the Hag Fold estate rented by the Police Authority to accommodate police officers. It was semi-detached with two doubles and one single bedroom and gardens to the front and rear. It was situated in a cul-de-sac on the farthest side of the estate away from the police station. Renting houses on the outskirts of an estate effectively provided additional visible uniformed police patrols by officers travelling between their homes and the police station at the start and finish of each shift.

A local shop owner, from whom we had purchased dining and bedroom suites for our new home, loaned us his furniture van to collect a number of items we had stored at Kathleen's parents' home. He explained that the local police had been so kind and considerate to him and his family at the time of his mother's death that he tried to return the kindness whenever he could. That I should benefit from the past actions of officers I did not know and had never met taught me an early and important lesson about human behaviour, which I never forgot. One of the sergeants actually drove the van for us to Hope as I didn't have a driving licence; a good example of how we all mucked in to help each other. He did allow me pay for the petrol.

We gradually got the house and garden straight in time for Debra to be born on 8th July, 1963, in The Firs Maternity Home in Leigh. We owned very little, just enough basic furniture to manage with, but no luxuries like fitted carpets or a TV set. All her baby things were second hand, including her pram, carry-cot, bath and play-pen. Taking her to see either set of grandparents involved complex combinations of train and bus journeys with the pram or the carry-cot.

We were very lucky in our immediate next door neighbours. Tommy Banks was a Fireman employed by the Lancashire County Fire Brigade. He and his wife, Norah, devout Catholics, had three children of their own and were very good to us in a number of ways. Over time they became almost like surrogate grand-parents to Debra. Although they were older than us, we soon became friends and learned a lot from them about running a home. By the time Stuart was born in March 1966 we were quite settled in Atherton and had made friends both in and out of the job. The midwife decided that Kathleen would have a home birth for Stuart and as soon as she realised I was a police officer she insisted that I be present at the birth, "purely for professional reasons" she said. To my great surprise and pleasure he was born on my birthday.

Kathleen and I attended Bolton Road Methodist Church whenever possible, shifts permitting, and got to know some of the congregation. On the few occasions when we were able to go to church together on a Sunday evening, we would leave the children in their night clothes with Norah Banks who loved having them.

Chapter Nine

Post Probationary Policing

Once the two year probationary period had passed and your appointment as a constable had been confirmed, much more self-generated work was expected by both supervisors and colleagues. The atmosphere at Atherton Police Station was very supportive, other than towards those who failed to pull their weight. I received nothing but help from colleagues and especially two of the three sergeants who encouraged me to make the most of my educational background. The one exception was a particular senior constable, who went out of his way to cause trouble. He delighted in spreading false rumours and denigrating work I had done. He wasn't a member of my shift so I didn't have to work with him on a regular basis. I eventually concluded that he was jealous of my success in the promotion examinations and my good relationship with the DS. He had failed both the education and professional exams on several occasions and desperately wanted to be a detective, but feared that I might beat him to it.

On New Year's Day 1965 I arrived for the early shift at 5.45 a.m. It was bitterly cold and the night shift had already come in to de-frost prior to the hand-over. The colleague reporting with me was PC Walter Bowring, the senior constable on my shift. The night sergeant had finished at 2 a.m. and the day sergeant was not due to come on until 9 a.m. A worker who had just finished a night shift at one of the mills came into the station to report that he had found a man unconscious on the street and presumed he had had too much to drink the previous evening. Walter told me to go with the young man to see whether or not an ambulance would be needed. It was only a couple of hundred yards from the station and on arrival I could see that the man appeared to be dead.

His body was half on the footpath and half in the road with its head in a pool of congealed blood. There was no pulse or other sign of life. I could hardly believe my eyes, however, for the body was that of Ralph Carr, one of the three sergeants at our station. I sent the young man back to the station to fetch Walter and tell him who the dead man was. Walter duly arrived, took one look and confirmed that it was indeed Sgt Carr. He told me to guard the scene while he went back to the station to raise the alarm. It didn't take long for senior officers to arrive, the divisional commander and the head of CID together with a police surgeon. First thoughts were that he may have been assaulted and, as his body was found about half way between his own house and that of his married girl-friend, both his wife and the girl-friend's husband were questioned. As the reporting officer I had to go to the post mortem along with the head of CID and the divisional commander. I felt out of place with such senior ranks, but the pathologist directed all his remarks to me and I kept the official log of what occurred. In the end it transpired that he had had too much to drink on New Year's Eve, had fallen over on his way home, hitting his head on the edge of the kerb and had died from the impact. I later acted as one of the pall bearers at his funeral.

With just three years' service I was recommended for a driving course at force HQ as I had recently passed my civilian driving test. Passing this course meant that I went on to the rota of constables permitted to drive the police vehicle allocated to the sub-division, thereby widening my experience of dealing with different types of incidents.

One evening I was on duty in the police station when I received a 999 call from the licensee of a local pub to the effect that two men were fighting in the public bar and were smashing the place up. I couldn't contact either of the two foot patrol constables so I rang DHQ for mobile assistance to be told that all cars were busy. When I asked what I should do I was told to lock up the station and go and deal with the incident myself, which I did. I got there to find the fight still in progress with chairs and tables overturned and beer all over the floor. I told the two men to stop fighting and behave themselves which, to my complete amazement, they did. Moreover they apologised to the landlord and said they would pay for any damage caused. I couldn't believe my eyes or my ears. Was I truly such a commanding figure that my word in itself was sufficient to restore peace and tranquillity? Taking advantage of their compliance I told them that if they left immediately and went straight home they wouldn't hear any more about it. They couldn't get out of the pub quickly enough. The landlord expressed his thanks and offered me a beer, which I gratefully accepted. We chatted for a moment or two and then I left. That's when my naivety was brought home with a bang and I mean that literally. The two men were waiting for me outside, one either side of the pub door. As I turned to go back to the station, one grabbed me from behind and pinned my arms whilst the other started punching and kicking me about the head and body. I struggled as hard as I could but couldn't break free and was taking a real hammering when another man came out of the pub. He grabbed the one who was holding me and restrained him leaving me free to tackle the other. "Two on to one isn't fair" was all he said while he waited to see what would happen next. I managed to subdue my assailant and handcuffed him whereon my helper offered to bring the other one with me to the police station. We got them both there and the four of us were together inside when the door opened and my two colleagues rushed in, having just heard what had happened. I was dishevelled and completely out of breath, my helmet had been knocked off and was lying somewhere in the street, my tie was undone, my ear was torn, my face was bleeding and I looked a real mess. They went straight for the man who had helped me. I had to intervene and explain what had happened. They refused to believe me at first, saying I must be confused because the man I claimed had helped me was a well-known criminal with a string of convictions as long as both arms including assault on police. I managed to convince them that he really had come to my aid so they reluctantly let him go. As if to confirm what they had said, he rolled up both his sleeves revealing his convictions which he did have tattooed on his arms. I thanked him profusely and he reiterated that he had no love for the police, but I'd been fair to the men in the pub and two against one just isn't right. A couple of weeks later he was arrested and jailed for trying to brain one of my colleagues with a spade after being caught stealing from a building site. When the sergeant finally arrived he refused to let me charge the two men with assault on police saying that it was the drink that had caused them to act as they did, so the appropriate charge was drunk and disorderly. Conviction for assault on police would have resulted in custodial sentences and they were not intrinsically bad men he said. I wasn't happy and protested vehemently but he prevailed and at court the following week they were fined £10 each. I got a card from each of them at Christmas wishing me well.

Promotion Examinations

Knowing that I could not even sit the promotion exam to sergeant until I had completed four years' service, I was determined not to waste time and repeat my Goldsmiths' fiasco, so I enrolled on a newly advertised evening study course offered by Wigan & District Mining & Technical College. The curriculum covered the syllabus for the professional element of the Police Promotion exams and the target audience was serving police officers. Lectures were given by college staff and local members of the legal profession. I had to pay my own enrolment fees and often exchanged shifts so as not to miss any of the classes. The course ran for two academic terms and I attended every single session. Police promotion exams at that time were set and marked nationally under the aegis of the Civil Service Commission. Held twice yearly in February and November, the syllabus was a public document and previous years' papers were readily available. That pilot course was so successful that in subsequent years the force gave permission for students to attend in duty time and for their course fees to be reimbursed.

I duly made application to sit the February 1966 exam, knowing that I would have completed four years' service in the January. As the force had to pay an entry fee for each candidate, frivolous applications had to be weeded out. My application was supported by the Divisional Commander, Chief Superintendent Humble, and was approved by HQ Personnel. It was unheard of at that time for one so junior in service to make such an application. To my great surprise I was also informed that Mr. Humble had recommended me for a crammer course to be held at the force training school prior to the actual exam. No-one from Leigh Division had previously been recommended and it was generally held that selection was a virtual guarantee of success in the national exam. The course was of two weeks duration and consisted of lectures and discussion on the syllabus followed by advice on examination technique and answering papers from previous years which were then analysed and marked using the Civil Service Commission Markers' Guide. Naturally there was strong competition for places on the course and some degree of resentment among those who had not been successful. Of the fourteen students on the course only three of us had fewer than six years' service, the remainder having ten or more. I was the only one with barely four years in the job.

The exam itself consisted of three papers of one and a half hours duration and was held at the Town Hall in Bury. When it came to the actual questions I found them relatively straightforward and encountered nothing for which I had failed to prepare. Some weeks later I was told to contact the Chief Superintendent at DHQ. On ringing his office I was informed that I had not only passed the exam but had come in the top two hundred in the country, thereby qualifying for interview at the Home Office in London for the recently introduced Accelerated Promotion Scheme at the Police College. I had read about the 'Johnson Scheme' in the 'Police Review' magazine and had commented to Kathleen that it was not for the likes of us. How wrong can you be!

I attended Horseferry House in London where, for just over three quarters of an hour, I was grilled by a panel of two Chief Constables and a senior Home Office official. Panel members would probably have said rigorously interviewed, but grilling is what it felt like at the time. I must have satisfied them because I was subsequently called to attend the next stage in the process, a three day Extended Interview (EI) selection procedure at Eastbourne. Those three days of EI left me physically and emotionally drained, having undergone a host of written test papers, group exercises and a succession of individual interviews with panels of Chief Constables and highly qualified non-Service personnel. I felt I had done justice to myself but was surprised to learn that some of the other candidates had been coached by their various forces for the three day EI procedure. I went in cold; the force had helped me to prepare for the promotion exams, but not the follow up; that was completely down to me.

Nevertheless, I was successful and was selected to attend the fifth Special Course (SC) at the Police College commencing in September 1966. It was a twelve-month course to prepare successful students for accelerated promotion to the rank of Chief Inspector. As I would not have attained five years' service by the start of the course, I would be promoted to temporary sergeant in order to attend. I was only the second Lancashire officer to be selected for the SC which had only been inaugurated in the year I joined the police.

Following my initial elation at being selected I experienced a sense of deep concern, largely about the costs of attending the course, despite the pay rise on promotion. Students were required to be in possession of a series of legal and other textbooks, a formal dinner suit and blazer and flannels for official visits when uniform was not appropriate. My salary at that time was in the region of £750 per annum and we had two young children. We just could not afford to buy all those things. I explained this to Chief Superintendent Humble who acknowledged my concerns, but insisted that I had to take up the place for the sake of my future career.

His first response was to arrange for the force to buy the textbooks which, at the end of the course, would be placed in the training school library at Stanley Grange and thus become available for future students. He also gave me his own blazer to wear for the duration of the course and actually had it altered to fit me, with the force crest sewn on to the breast pocket, all at his own expense. He also persuaded the manager of a local tailor's shop to allow me to buy a dinner suit on credit over twelve months. His final act was to ask his deputy to visit our home and explain to Kathleen why it was so important that I attend. Not only was Chief Superintendent Humble thoughtful and generous, but Chief Inspector Ball, his deputy, followed suit. He visited Kathleen whilst I was away on the course and even drove her down to Hampshire for one of the formal Guest Nights. I don't think that many senior officers would have acted in that way and I owe a great debt of gratitude to both men. Much later, after his own promotion to Chief Superintendent, Max Ball told me that together they had recognised my potential to become an effective senior officer and were determined to do all they could to assist me.

Leonard family group – 1949

Aerial view of Storthes Hall Hospital

National Service – 1958

No 1 District Police Training Centre, Bruche – March 1962

Wedding – September 1962

Family in Swanwick 1980

Pleasley Colliery

QPM Ceremony – 1987

CC Humberside - 1992

Chapter Ten

The Special Course, Bramshill

The Fifth Special Course (SCV) started in September 1966 when sixty (fifty-eight male and two female) apprehensive and newly promoted sergeants from all over England and Wales arrived at Bramshill House, a Grade One listed Jacobean mansion set in its own grounds in the Hampshire countryside. Sixty was the maximum number for the course but not every place had been filled on the previous four courses. It was widely rumoured that the Home Office had only agreed to fill this course following political pressure by the national leaders of the Police Federation.

One of the problems faced by the Police College in the 1960s and subsequent decades was a lack of self-confidence and clarity about its role. Its prestige had been established by the purchase of the Bramshill estate and by one of Her Majesty's Inspectors of Constabulary (HMIC) being placed in charge. What it lacked, however, was clear role definition. Was it to be a university for the Police Service or a management training college? Would it become a centre of excellence for an elite officer cadre or a liberal studies college for the many? Liberal studies occupied almost half the syllabus of every course at Bramshill, principally taught by academic staff, many of whom at that time were Oxbridge educated former colonial administrators. Fortunately for students it was the academic staff which had the final say in the awarding of university scholarships. Adding to the confusion over its professional standing was a constant sense of insecurity about social status, demonstrated by attempts to mimic neighbouring military establishments such as the Staff College at Camberley and the Royal Military Academy at Sandhurst. Much of Bramshill's routine and nomenclature aped that of the military; formal mess nights; classes being called syndicates; instructors being known as syndicate directors and academic staff having a lower status than police staff. Even as a new student it was obvious to me that the social class of the majority of potential senior police officers was deemed to be inferior to that of commissioned officers in the armed forces. Much was made of the fact that the absence of direct officer entry meant that senior police officers were promoted from the ranks and did not hold a Queen's commission. A former editor of the Daily Telegraph summed it up neatly when he told an annual conference of the Association of Chief Police Officers (ACPO); "You're working class. You're not chaps."

Our course itself, as well as its members, seemed to be at the heart of these uncertainties. We were heartily sick of constantly being told that it was the course which was special, not us, and we were treated more like schoolchildren than serving police sergeants. The course director, Chief Superintendent Ridge of the Liverpool City Police, was totally unsuited to hold that position and should never have been appointed as he did not believe in any form of accelerated promotion and made his views known. Fortunately for us he played no part in our tuition, but made his presence felt through a host of petty restrictions about behaviour and discipline. In stark contrast to all the other courses at Bramshill, SC students had to undergo military style foot drill on the square following morning parade plus compulsory physical training sessions and weekly cross country runs, despite the fact that we were much younger, fitter and more active than any other group of students at the college.

The police service at that time was subject to a forty-eight hour week, so Saturday mornings were an integral part of the timetable for each course. That meant that only those officers who lived within easy travelling distance could go home at weekends. The rest of us had to manage with one long weekend a month, from 1pm Friday to midnight Sunday. College life, therefore, extended to evenings and weekends with social activities organised by staff and students. Societies and clubs included debating, history, play reading, choir, music appreciation, chess, cinema, stage shows plus most indoor and outdoor sports, both team and individual. An additional restriction placed on SC students was compulsory sport on Saturday afternoons at which attendance by non-players was obligatory. With no Methodist church nearby, I attended Anglican services in the college chapel or in the village of Eversley whenever I could.

Only being able to get home once a month, arriving in Atherton about 5 p.m. on a Friday and having to leave again around 5 p.m. on Sunday, placed a great deal of strain on Kathleen. She had to manage with two small children, no car and no telephone and more than sixty miles away from both sets of parents and other family members. On my arrival home she would have the washing machine ready for my dirty laundry which then had to be ironed by the time I had to leave. Stuart in particular was a poor sleeper as a baby, often waking up during the night and making a good night's rest almost impossible to achieve. I don't honestly know how she would have coped had it not been for the Banks family next door. Norah and Tommy were unbelievably supportive while I was away. One of my SCV colleagues was unable to complete the course as his wife had a nervous breakdown so he returned home to be with her, declining the offer of a place on the next course. That could so easily have been Kathleen and I owe her a tremendous debt of gratitude for her perseverance and fortitude.

The professional studies modules of the course covered the syllabus for the promotion examination to Inspector but went into much greater detail on the organisation and administration of the police. Weekly tests were followed by exams at the end of each term, in which a minimum of seventy per cent had to be achieved. Failure in any one exam would result in the denial of a graduation certificate at the end of the course, a significant 'incentive' as SC graduates were exempted from sitting the national promotion examination to Inspector.

There seemed to be an almost permanent debate as to whether or not the liberal and professional studies aspects of the course should be taught in discrete blocs or interspersed throughout a course. The liberal studies syllabus included history, sociology, economics, philosophy and English literature. Both methods were tried on our course, which did not always work to our benefit.

At the end of the course five students were refused graduation certificates, having failed to reach the seventy per cent mark in one of the tests. This caused a great deal of anger as it was felt that the decision was politically motivated in response to the earlier pressure from the Police Federation to accept the maximum number of students. I graduated as best student and was awarded a university scholarship starting in the following September.

On returning to Lancashire my temporary promotion was made substantive and it was decided that to broaden my experience I should perform six months duty as a patrol sergeant, followed by three months as a traffic sergeant and three months as a detective sergeant before being promoted to the rank of Inspector and taking up my university scholarship. I was called to HQ for an interview with the Chief Constable who informed me that I would not need to return to duty during university vacations as some other forces had insisted, but was to use the time to keep ahead of my studies. In preceding years only University College, London, and the London School of Economics & Political Science (LSE) had been prepared to take Bramshill scholars, but other universities were now following suit. A colleague and I were interviewed for the solitary place offered by Selwyn College, Cambridge. Although the selection panel was impressed by my interview, they said they felt that the College would not be able to cope with an undergraduate student who was married with two young children and would not live in hall, so my younger, unmarried colleague was offered the place. In contrast the LSE welcomed mature students and offered me a place without reserve.

Barbara Castle, when Minister for Transport, introduced the breathalyser to reduce the number of deaths and injuries caused by drink-driving. The breathalyser instrument itself was awkward to use. More critical legally was the procedure to be adopted at the police station following an arrest. For the first time ever an accused was required by law to provide a sample of blood. Refusal to provide a sample became an offence carrying the same penalty as a positive test. This had caused much debate in parliament over whether, under English law, an individual could be required to self-incriminate. On the day the law came into force I arrested a driver at the scene of an accident following a positive breath test, the very first in Lancashire and one of the first in the country. At the police station I gave one of the new blood test kits to the police surgeon. He said it was both unsafe and unhygienic and refused to use the instrument in the kit to obtain a small sample of blood from the ball of a suspect's finger. Instead he took a syringe from his medical bag and extracted blood from a vein in the man's arm. The motorist didn't object as he was unaware of the recommended procedure and subsequently pleaded guilty at court. I had to warn the doctor that if the legal profession got to know what he had done then the case would be thrown out on appeal. For weeks afterwards I got phone calls from all over the country asking advice on how I had dealt with the new procedures.

Nevertheless my year as a sergeant in the three departments passed very quickly and I was flattered when the head of CID offered me a permanent position as Detective Inspector following my three months in CID. He could not understand why I declined and chose to go to university instead.

In September 1968 we moved as a family into a Metropolitan Police flat in East Dulwich ready for my undergraduate course in Sociology at the LSE.

Chapter Eleven

London School of Economics & Political Science

The three years at the LSE proved to be significant in my future career. I made it my habit to attend university between 9 a.m. and 6 p.m. daily from Monday to Friday, keeping weekends for the family whenever possible. I maintained that schedule throughout term time and vacations, only taking time off equivalent to my police annual leave entitlement. As the first member of my family to go to university, I was determined not to waste this second chance.

I was extremely fortunate in the quality of the academic staff teaching at LSE during my time there, many of whom enjoyed international reputations. I took full advantage and attended a range of lectures, many of which were not directly related to my course. One of the reasons I chose the LSE was the fact that about forty per cent of its students were classified as 'mature.' I arrived to find a number of police officers already at LSE on Bramshill scholarships, mainly from the Inspectors' course. They quickly became a good source of information and advice about university life. Within my own year group I gravitated to a circle of acquaintances who were also married; some self-financing, one on a Civil Service bursary and a couple more on Trades Union scholarships. As married students we found a greater degree of shared interest between ourselves, regardless of age, than we ever could with single students.

One professor in the Politics faculty described me in a seminar as "the archetypical upwardly mobile working class student." When asked by another student to justify the statement he said, "It's easy. He attends every lecture and seminar, completes every assignment, hands all his essays in on time and I can even read his handwriting." I wasn't quite sure whether or not it was meant as a compliment.

1968, the year of my arrival, was a year of student protest around the world, mainly against the continuing war in Vietnam. Students across Europe and the United States staged sit-ins, occupied their universities and colleges and in France almost brought down the government of President de Gaulle. London saw anti-war demonstrations outside the American Embassy in Grosvenor Square. LSE was no exception and the Students' Union cleverly co-opted its police students to act as legal and tactical advisors when considering direct action and as security officers for special meetings. Nevertheless, despite sit-ins, occupations, closures and demonstrations, academic work progressed and after my three years study I was awarded an honours degree in sociology. I was told by a senior member of the Sociology faculty that my final paper in Criminology was adjudged to have been the best paper submitted by an undergraduate student for many years.

Family Life in London

Outside of university, our three years in London was mind-blowing for all the family. Debra and Stuart attended a multi-ethnic, multi-cultural school for the first time and we all benefited from living in the heart of a multi-racial community. Just round the corner from our flat was Barry Road Methodist Church, to which we transferred our membership. The minister had previously worked under Reverend Dr Soper at Kingsway Hall and followed Soper's style of ministry. The church was really welcoming and we made friendships which lasted for many years. One lady told Kathleen they had been praying for a family like ours to join them. Kathleen became a Sunday school teacher and I helped to lead the Youth Club.

Within the church we forged a deep and lasting bond with the Lakey family. Rod, Bertha and their two children were political refugees from South Africa, classified under apartheid as 'Cape Coloureds.' Members of an affluent and well educated middle class family, they had supported the dependants of political prisoners through their local Methodist church. "We could do no less as Christians" they observed. This had brought them into direct conflict with the South African State which labelled Rod as a communist and threatened him with 'banning' and imprisonment. They managed to flee before he was arrested and settled in East Dulwich. They were unable to return to their native land until the apartheid regime had been replaced. Rod became the senior accountant at Kings College Hospital and Bertha secured a secretarial appointment at the Foreign Office. From them we learned far more about their native land and the evils of apartheid and racism than I had ever encountered in my earlier student links with the Anti-Apartheid movement. We also discovered that when members of a Christian community actually put their principles into practice, such action is frequently labelled by their opponents as 'bringing politics into religion,' something of which I was accused at a later date.

Chapter Twelve

Return to Lancashire

On our return from London we were allocated a police house within walking distance of the police HQ complex. We enrolled Debra and Stuart at the local junior school where a large proportion of the pupils were the children of police officers working at HQ. Kathleen learned to drive as she felt the car was wasting money by standing idle because I walked to work each day. We transferred our church membership to Central Methodist Church, Lune Street, in Preston where I became one of the youth leaders. Our youth club was multi-racial and opened six nights a week. We deliberately encouraged teenagers to join us who had been banned from other clubs. We welcomed any and every-one so long as they behaved themselves on our premises, which most of them did for most of the time. In due course I was appointed as one of the church stewards. At home I also hosted and led a monthly discussion group for church members and adherents.

We moved house twice more in the same locality, first to a larger police house and then into our own property after the restriction on police officers purchasing their own homes was lifted. Kathleen took a job in Preston at a factory making sweets and chocolates and regaled us with stories of the people who worked there and what they got up to.

We felt we had something to offer so in 1972 applied to Social Services to become foster parents and following interview were accepted. Our first foster child was a seven year old boy whose father was in and out of jail on a regular basis and whose mother had mental problems which meant that from time to time she had to be hospitalised. Whenever this occurred, her children were taken into care. Social workers described him to us as hyperactive, naughty, wilfully disobedient and a bed-wetter.

He was indeed insecure as his early life had been anything but stable. Nevertheless he settled in well and our own children were wonderfully understanding with him. He went to school with them and became just another member of our family. He eventually stopped bed-wetting and, through a school health check, we found out that what social workers had identified as naughtiness and disobedience was due to a hearing defect which was capable of being remedied. We grew to love him and resented it when social services abruptly removed him without consultation after almost a year with us. All we were told was that he and his siblings, whom he hardly knew, were to be placed in a children's home to keep them together as a family. With no explanations, we felt as if we were being punished. Our second placement was a lovely young girl who only stayed with us for six weeks whilst her mother was recovering from a difficult time in childbirth.

I returned to police work at HQ as duty officer in charge of the force control room working a three shift system. This gave me my first opportunity to experience the implications of policing a large geographical area and managing the allocation of resources, both staff and materiel. Control room was seen as a plum job with a great deal of competition for the Inspectors' posts as they gave direct access to the most senior officers of the force, including the Chief Constable. One of the responsibilities of the duty officer on the night shift was to prepare a summary for each of the chief officers of all the significant occurrences in the county over the past twenty-four hours, including relevant reports in the local and national press. Determining what might, or might not, be relevant was something I found interesting and was surprised to learn that I was the first Inspector ever to have asked for feedback about the usefulness of the summaries I had compiled.

At this time in the Lancashire Constabulary's history, applicants for promotion to chief inspector and above had first of all to be recommended by their divisional commander or head of department, followed by an interview with a promotion board chaired by an Assistant Chief Constable (ACC). After the completion of the interview, candidates were graded from A to D. An A grade usually intimated promotion within twelve months, subject to vacancies, whereas a D grade indicated the candidate was not yet ready or was unsuitable for further advancement.

For four successive years, from 1972 to 1975, I was awarded an A grade, yet officers with a B or a C were promoted. At a HQ social function, an ACC, who had had far too much to drink, apologised to Kathleen mumbling that they were waiting to find exactly the right position for me. Others privately told me that, as a penance for my three years at LSE, I would have to wait for the same length of time that I had been at university before being considered.

In 1973 I was drafted into the Organisation Department to form part of a new team tasked with preparing for the reorganisation of police forces across the entire North West Region. The Lancashire Constabulary was the largest force in the country outside London at that time, but was to be reduced to less than half its size in both geography and staffing by the creation of new Metropolitan counties based on Liverpool and Manchester and the ceding of the Furness area to the new combined county of Cumbria. The team of one superintendent, two chief inspectors, two inspectors, two sergeants, one constable and a civilian finance specialist reported directly to one of the ACCs.

My particular role was planning the internal structure for the new Lancashire; how many geographical divisions and sub-divisions would be required; what would be their staffing requirements; how adequate for those purposes were existing buildings and plant and what Home Office permissions would be needed to achieve a successful outcome? It entailed a steep learning curve as we had to ensure that normal departmental functions were maintained in addition to our new responsibilities. One of the incidental tasks I was given was to write speeches for the Chief Constable on the occasions he was called upon to speak professionally rather than at social functions. It was frustrating in that he always used what I had written but never offered a single word of feedback, critical or complimentary.

The department was led by Chief Superintendent Goldsborough, a Cambridge graduate who was ideally placed in that role. He had asked for me to be transferred to his department following conversations we'd had over lunch in the dining room. I was told he saw me as a potential successor. He gave his support to a paper I produced recommending that the force adopt a formal staff appraisal scheme, but the concept proved too difficult for the head of personnel to accept. What I learned in Organisation, however, was worth its weight in gold in later years.

St Annes Sub-division

After reorganisation in 1974 I returned to operational policing as Deputy Sub-divisional Commander at St Annes on the Fylde coast. The sub-division covered the two seaside resorts of Lytham and St Annes, traditional but popular holiday destinations, housing a high proportion of retired people. It struck me as a sad reflection on society that during the night a patrol would respond to a burglar alarm activation only to be met at the door of the house or flat with a cup of tea and piece of cake prepared by a lonely and elderly widow desperate for some form of human contact. I was delighted that my staff tended to treat such calls with compassion rather than reporting them as deliberate false alarms. I enjoyed being back in direct contact with the public and relished my time there, particularly pitting my wits against defence solicitors in the Magistrates' Court.

Two very different incidents stick in my memory, the first soon after my arrival. The British Open Golf Championship was being hosted by the Royal Lytham and St Annes Golf Club and, under the guise of monitoring crowd-behaviour, I walked part of the course with Jack Nicklaus, a real gentleman. The second incident was much more memorable and involved the comedian, Les Dawson. An exclusive and expensive housing development was being built in St Annes, locally known at the time as 'Millionaires' Row', and word got around that Les Dawson was buying one of the houses. Some of the other purchasers felt that his presence would lower the tone and hence the price of their properties and started a petition to prevent his purchase. In the event they failed, he bought a house and moved in. That's when I became involved. It was late at night and I heard a call over the radio about a suspicious vehicle on the new estate. I got there to find one of my constables talking to a couple of men unloading a furniture removal van. They explained that they had been delayed en-route and would be there for some time. Then Les Dawson came out of the house, took one look at us and "I've got the kettle on, are you coming in for a brew?" The sergeant and another constable arrived and we all went inside. Les said he'd had a very long day and was starving and asked if any chip shops were still open nearby. One of the PCs said he knew of one, so Dawson took out his wallet, gave the PC some money and said "Go and get fish and chips for everybody, if that's OK with you Inspector." When the fish and chips arrived we all searched around for something to sit on, packing cases and tea chests, and Les went round handing out mugs of tea and we all tucked in. Then it started. With a lap full of fish, chips and tea, he started telling stories which had us all in stitches. He went on for a couple of hours hardly pausing for breath. We could have listened all night enjoying the entertainment, but duty called, so we thanked him and reluctantly bade him goodnight.

Blackpool South Sub-division

My transfer in 1975 to the adjacent Blackpool South sub-division came as a complete surprise. The County Borough of Blackpool had only become part of the Lancashire Constabulary following the amalgamations of police forces in 1969. Its last Chief Constable had subsequently been appointed Chief of the combined force but acted as though he had never left the borough. The attitude of staff there was still very parochial, almost as if amalgamation had never taken place. I was the first county officer to be posted into the former borough and when I was shown round on my first day I was shocked to be told "This is the Borough boundary and over there is the County."

Nevertheless it was a valuable experience. I had never paraded as many officers on a shift as I encountered at South. I seemed to have more sergeants than we had constables at Atherton. In particular I continued to enjoy prosecuting in the Magistrates' Court. At St Annes I had been used to receiving files in good time to prepare before arriving in court, but in Blackpool was expected to prosecute from files I hadn't even had time to read. A further novelty was being asked by the magistrates to join them when they retired to consider their verdict in case there was something that couldn't be said in open court. My declining of their offer was not kindly received and did my reputation no favours.

It was also in Blackpool that I had my first real encounter with improper influence or corrupt behaviour. I was on patrol with one of my sergeants when we were approached by a member of the public complaining that a particular street was completely blocked by illegally parked cars, to such an extent that emergency services vehicles would be unable to gain access. We went to the scene where I asked the sergeant to get a constable or traffic warden to move them on or ticket them immediately. He became embarrassed and told me that it wouldn't do any good because the owner of the premises outside which they were parked would just get the Chief Constable to cancel the tickets as they were in the same Masonic lodge and it had happened before. The owner did come out and brazenly told me to mind my own business or he would have me transferred. I made sure that the vehicles were ticketed and, sure enough, all the Fixed Penalty Notices were subsequently cancelled by the Chief.

Chapter Thirteen

Promotion to Chief Inspector

In late September 1975 as I arrived for duty, a PC offered me congratulations on my promotion to Chief Inspector, it having been announced at his Masonic Lodge the previous evening. I wasn't officially notified until the following day when I learned that I was to take charge of a new branch, Community Relations, but would be its sole member. I received no guidance, instructions or advice but was told to set something up and get it running. I was given an office and allocated a mileage allowance for using my own car but nothing else, so I had to write my own script. I found it ironic because two years previously, whilst in Organisation at HQ, I had recommended that the force create such a branch in order to address the needs of policing a multi-racial and multi-cultural society. The proposal had been rejected at the time as being both unnecessary and a waste of resources.

My original paper had envisaged the establishment of a properly resourced and staffed branch, but as that was not going to happen, my first priority was to try to find out where my new branch would be located in the force organisational structure and to whom I would be accountable in the chain of command. My requests caused some consternation at HQ as nobody had any idea of how to respond. Personnel couldn't help as they had not been consulted. Eventually I was told that Community Relations would be a stand-alone branch and if I was desperate for professional advice then I should go to a Superintendent who just happened to have an office in the same building as me. So in a complete policy and information vacuum I began my time as the Lancashire Constabulary's first Community Relations Officer. At least I was clear about my job title.

I then had to learn how to navigate my way through the politics of the race relations industry at both national and local levels and try to determine which of the various professional bodies would be most likely to provide reliable advice for an absolute newcomer. I managed to contact Nadine Peppard, a race relations advisor at the Home Office, who could not have been more helpful. I spent what seemed like an eternity with her on the telephone over the next few days. She suggested whom I ought to try to get to know at both the Race Relations Board and the Community Relations Commission, warning me not to get caught up in the political tension between the two bodies. She strongly advised me to concentrate on establishing good contacts and working relationships at the local level before doing anything else. I gratefully followed her advice.

By the mid-1970s the new Lancashire Constabulary's population had changed dramatically. Work in the cotton industry had attracted people to its mills from across the Indian sub-continent, settling in the north-eastern belt of towns which runs from Preston through Blackburn to Burnley and the Yorkshire border. These workers from Pakistani, Bengali and Indian communities spoke a variety of languages and adhered to different religious faiths and cultural traditions. A much smaller Afro-Caribbean community had mainly settled in the Preston and Leyland areas.

My first and most important local contact was recommended by a senior youth officer for the Preston District Council whom I had come to know through my voluntary work as a youth leader at Lune Street Methodist church. He put me in touch with Sayeed Ahmed, the full-time Community Relations Officer for Preston who really kick-started my learning-curve. Sayeed arranged for me to meet his opposite numbers from the other main towns and facilitated my introduction into their various religious and cultural groups. Through them I became an ex-officio member of each of the separate and independent Community Relations Councils across the force area.

It soon became clear that my new job required me to address issues from two separate perspectives, external and internal. I had to represent the police to communities with little or no experience of policing as an impartial public service and, on the other hand, to attempt to educate police officers themselves. A key function of my role was to introduce a training programme for serving officers whose factual knowledge about the different groups living among us was almost non-existent and among whom myths abounded and prejudice against other cultures and religions was widespread. My main disappointment was that the training could not be extended to include senior officers. Both the RRB and the CRC provided excellent source materials for training purposes.

Early in 1977 my attention was drawn to a Home Officer Circular inviting applications for a new national training course for recently appointed police community liaison officers to be held at the Derbyshire Constabulary HQ. The syllabus of the four week long course seemed to be so relevant that I submitted an application to attend. Shortly afterwards I received a telephone call from the Superintendent in charge of training in Derbyshire. He explained that the structure of the course required the appointment of two external syndicate directors and, from the details I had provided on my application form, he felt that I would be more suited for that role than as a student. I suggested he write to my Chief Constable asking for my participation, which he did, and I attended as a visiting syndicate director. The pilot course was a tremendous success, I learned a great deal and the Home Office agreed to continue to sponsor it on an annual basis with all expenses attracting Home Office grant.

In June, 1977, on returning from a two week family holiday in France I found the latest copy of the 'Police Review' in the porch. In the magazine a vacancy for the post of Superintendent in charge of training for the Derbyshire Constabulary was advertised. For the first time in the history of the police in England and Wales, only graduates were invited to apply. As Derbyshire is Kathleen's home county, we held a family discussion after which it was decided that I should apply. The closing date, however, was only three days hence and applications had to be submitted through the Chief Constable. That evening I telephoned Superintendent Charlie Cooper, who had known me since I was a constable, at his home to ask for his advice. He told me to go straight to my office and complete an application. He then drafted a letter for the Chief Constable's signature. With the deadline in mind and being only too well aware of our Chief's blinkered attitude, he decided to bypass him and took the letter of recommendation, with my application, to the Deputy Chief Constable, Mr Moody. Stressing the need for urgency he asked Mr Moody to sign the letter and forward both documents without delay to the Chief Constable of Derbyshire, which he did.

I was duly called for interview at Derbyshire HQ before a panel consisting of the Chief Constable, the Deputy Chief Constable and one of the two Assistant Chief Constables. All three panel members were Freemasons and, of the six candidates interviewed, I was the only one who was not a Mason. Fortunately I knew nothing of this at the time. After the interviews were over, I was called back in and was offered the job. The Chief Constable further explained that he had received Home Office approval for the post to be upgraded to Chief Superintendent in twelve months' time so, provided that I lived up to their expectations, I would be promoted again to that rank.

My success engendered a variety of responses back in Lancashire. The Chief Constable neither spoke to me nor offered his congratulations, whereas Mr Moody, the Deputy Chief, sent for me to wish me well and offered any assistance he could give. My friends were delighted, saying so publicly whereas others, for their own reasons, called me a traitor for wanting to leave Lancashire.

Later that year the Lancashire Chief Constable was suspended from duty and subsequently dismissed following an investigation by Her Majesty's Inspectorate of Constabulary (HMIC) into his conduct for a number of offences including interfering with prosecutions on behalf of Masonic colleagues and abuse of authority. I cannot help but compare him unfavourably with his two predecessors as Chief and his fall brought shame on a proud force.

Chapter Fourteen

Transfer to the Derbyshire Constabulary

Moving one's family from one county to another is never easy, but in this case the timing seemed to work in our favour. We sold our house quickly and the children were able to start their new school from the beginning of the autumn term. We initially occupied a police house in Shirland, using it as a base from which to scour the area to find a property to buy. We eventually decided on a house in Swanwick, a former mining village between Alfreton and Ripley where we remained for almost eight years. It was quite a surprise to be told that the National Coal Board possessed the mineral rights to our garden.

We transferred our membership to Swanwick Methodist Church, one of three places of worship in the village. After settling in, I hosted and led a discussion group at the church, the success of which caused the minister to ask me to help out the circuit by occasionally taking services on Sundays when there was a shortage of lay preachers. I developed a good working relationship with the Anglican vicar, whom I subsequently persuaded to become Chaplain to the Training School. Through him I became involved with the Derby Diocesan Education Officer who offered to help with staff development for my own team.

The surrounding area was made up of small industrial villages, very closely knit with a great deal of inter-marriage. We were warned by a neighbour; "If you scratch a …….. (a local surname), the entire village will bleed." Many of the inhabitants had never lived anywhere else and had little understanding of 'comers-in' with different experiences of life. It is never easy to gain acceptance in a small community, but we committed ourselves to the locality and made new family friends across the age range.

Through the church youth group, Debra became involved with the Methodist Association of Youth Clubs (MAYC), being first of all chosen as Personality Girl for the Nottingham and Derbyshire District and then the national winner. She became chair of the MAYC National Members' Council and subsequently a Methodist representative to the British Youth Council, in which role she attended an international Youth Congress in Moscow where she met her future husband for the first time.

Training School

I took up my new position as head of training on 1st September 1977 and, in complete contrast to my promotion to Chief Inspector in Lancashire, received a detailed briefing about the Derbyshire Constabulary, its training department, my new role and what was expected from me. I also learned something about my new Chief Constable and why I, a non-Mason, had been selected in preference to the others. It had been a well-qualified short list of candidates, but two factors had swayed the Chief Constable in my direction. He recognised in me the potential to become a chief officer and knew that I would have to move on to achieve that, which meant I would not block the rank in Derbyshire for too long. In addition, as chair of ACPO's Training Committee and a member of the national Police Training Council, he wanted to encourage closer cooperation with European police forces. My fluency in French, coupled with an adequate knowledge of German, would allow him to use me to achieve that ambition.

Having spent four weeks at the Training School as a visiting syndicate director I had become familiar with the physical layout and had got to know some of the staff, so I did not appear on the scene as a completely unknown entity. I later found out that some of the staff had run a book on who was most likely to be their new boss and I had been their odds on favourite.

The campus, part of the recently built police HQ complex, included dormitory blocks containing 120 individual study-bedrooms; a suite of class and seminar rooms each fully equipped with the latest educational technology built into what was known as a teaching wall; a TV production studio for making films, broadcasting to classrooms and conducting media interview training; a multi-purpose sports hall; a small library; a social centre and bar; staff and administrative offices and separate VIP bedrooms for visiting lecturers. The prospectus offered both residential and day courses addressing needs from the purely local through to regional, national and international levels. The student population included teenaged cadets at the start of their police careers through to experienced chief inspectors and the curriculum covered all aspects of general and specialist policing duties with significant teaching input from external academics.

Prior to my appointment, overseas students had come mainly from African Commonwealth countries funded by the British Council. I was tasked with attracting a wider range of mid to senior ranking officers from within the UK and across Europe and the Middle East, without reducing the existing student pool. In preparation for this I was able to negotiate academic accreditation for our management courses from the University of Nottingham and Trent Polytechnic (later Nottingham Trent University). Eventually I was able to widen our catchment area to include students from France, Belgium, Denmark, Jordan, Saudi Arabia, Tanzania, Malawi, Zambia, Canada and Australia.

I had been in post for just a few months when one of my sergeants asked to see me in private in my office. He didn't know how to broach the subject and was quite embarrassed. Eventually, plucking up courage, he said that he could not understand why I behaved so differently from all the other senior officers he had worked for. I asked him to give me an example. "You are not at all rank-conscious," he said "you treat people with consideration and I'm not the only one who has noticed. Why are you like that?" It was my turn to be embarrassed as I wasn't sure how to respond. "Perhaps it's because I'm a Christian and see all people for what they are, my brothers and sisters," I finally offered. His face broke into a big smile of relief, "Oh! That explains it completely. Thank you, Sir," he said and left.

In early 1978 the Chief Constable nominated me to represent him at Interpol HQ in Paris at a conference for heads of European police training schools. The aim of the conference was to examine the feasibility of harmonising police training methods across the European Economic Community through wider and better use of the latest educational technology. Two Home Office (HO) nominees joined me in the UK team and I was surprised to learn that neither could speak a single word of French or indeed any other European language. Simultaneous translation facilities during the conference rendered such things unnecessary I was told. This worked to my advantage as they left me alone for most of the time and I was able to use the coffee breaks and lunch times to meet and talk with some of my European opposite numbers without HO staff breathing down my neck to see whether or not I was toeing the appropriate political line.

My knowledge of French and German enabled me to make a number of useful contacts which, in the fullness of time, led to French, Dutch, Belgian and Danish officers attending courses in Derbyshire to the great delight of my Chief Constable and the chief finance officer. More importantly, however, it resulted in the first of a series of exchanges of staff between the *Centre d'Application des Personnels en Uniforme* (CAPU), the Paris police training school, and my own. In 1979 three French officers from CAPU spent time with us in Derbyshire studying British training methods and techniques and later that year I took two members of my staff to Paris for a similar study of their system. It really tested my French when I was asked to lecture to a group of experienced sergeants on the differences between the French and English systems of policing and then take questions, but I managed to survive the experience.

In September 1978 I returned to Bramshill on Command Course Part I and was promoted to Chief Superintendent in December. Following my promotion, the Chief Constable invited Chief Inspector Bob Woodall from Gwent Police to transfer to Derbyshire on promotion to Superintendent to become my deputy. Bob subsequently told me about the Masonic connections. The key difference between my Derbyshire and Lancashire experiences lay in the fact that the Derbyshire Chief Constable was a man of great personal integrity, a quality I had rarely encountered among Freemasons. I was pressed, however, on a number of occasions to become a Mason, usually by subordinates in rank but consistently refused. I adversely compared the secrecy and self-serving nature of Freemasonry with the openness and concern for others of Christianity. I also felt membership to be incompatible with my oath of office as a constable.

Bob had been the runner-up candidate when I was appointed and his appointment allowed me to delegate to him certain functions which freed me to spend more time on career development programmes for other staff members. In this I came to rely heavily on the professional expertise of the Derby Diocesan Education officer who organised a series of seminars and courses for my colleagues. He, in turn, suggested to the manager of BBC Radio Derby that I might participate in their early morning 'Thought for the Day' programme. I was voice tested, accepted and became one of the regular presenters. I also gained the Chief's permission to open a chapel in the training school's social centre for a weekly non-denominational communion service conducted by the chaplain and for use at other times as a quiet room for students.

To maintain our accreditation with external academic partners I needed to improve and enlarge the library at the school to enable students to carry out research projects. I was delighted to secure funding for a professional librarian, the first in a provincial police force.

In the meantime the Chief Constable accepted an invitation from the publishing company Butterworths to edit and update the police text book, 'Moriarty's Police Law.' He asked me to assist him in the project along with the Deputy Chief and a fellow Chief Superintendent. Although the task was completed in good time, it proved to be the final edition of the book to be published.

The abysmally low level of police pay at this time had become a real source of dissatisfaction throughout the country. In 1976 the national leadership of the Police Federation had even canvassed members about whether they should seek the right to strike. I was appalled to learn that the sergeant who had asked the embarrassing question, a married man with three children, was claiming Family Income Supplement in order to make ends meet. In 1977 Prime Minister James Callaghan, a former parliamentary spokesman for the Police Federation, commissioned Lord Edmund-Davies to carry out an enquiry into police pay and conditions of service. Part I of his report was published in July the following year and recommended an across the board salary increase in the region of forty-five per cent. Astonishingly, the government accepted his report and agreed to increase police pay by forty per cent in two annual instalments of twenty per cent, the first in September 1978 and the second to come one year later. The first instalment was paid on time but the Labour Party then lost the 1979 general election. Mrs Thatcher, the new Prime Minister, brought forward the second instalment from September to May and claimed credit for the whole increase. That's politics for you.

Senior Command Course

In 1980 I applied for selection to the Senior Command Course (SCC) at the Police Staff College, a requirement for entry to the most senior ranks. The Chief Constable encouraged my application and, to broaden my operational command experience prior to the course, transferred me from the Training School to take charge of the Traffic Division. I attended the EI process at Eastbourne and was awarded a place on the course commencing in March 1981 along with twenty-four fellow UK officers and six from overseas. Following several unsuitable appointments to senior posts in a number of forces, the Home Office was endeavouring to persuade Police Authorities across the country not to appoint anyone as a Chief Officer in their force unless they were graduates of the Senior Command Course.

The publication of Part II of Lord Edmund-Davies' report, dealing with police representative and consultative procedures, caused the Staff College to require SCC students to undertake an examination of the role of Trades Unions and Staff Associations in the police of Canada, the United States, France, Germany and Holland. Because I could speak the language I was assigned to the team sent to Paris to study the French system. Only one other team member, Hugo Pike, was a French speaker. Although a series of official meetings had been scheduled, our visit took place during the 1981 Presidential election campaign, so very few high ranking civil servants or police commanders were prepared to speak to us on the record, knowing that much was about to change. However, our presence did permit the UK's Ambassador to host a cocktail party for senior French police officers at the British Embassy. In return we were invited to an informal reception at the Hotel de Matignon, official residence of the French Prime Minister. It was left to Hugo and me to use our personal contacts in the French police to enable us to successfully fulfil our mission.

The SCC syllabus was a mixture of compulsory and elective modules.

I was disappointed, but not surprised, when so few of my fellow students chose to study police administration and finance as an elective, opting instead for safe operational topics. To me that showed they had not yet grasped the magnitude of the change involved in being promoted from Chief Superintendent to Assistant Chief Constable. Predictably this made the transition more difficult for some of them when they did reach ACPO rank.

Chapter Fifteen

Promotion to Assistant Chief Constable

After graduating from the course I returned to Derbyshire and resumed my post as head of Traffic. The Chief Constable had retired and had been replaced by his Deputy. For a variety of reasons a further series of unanticipated changes in the Chief Officer team had occurred and an additional internal vacancy for an ACC was advertised. I leapt at the opportunity and immediately applied for it. HMIC supported my application and I was short-listed by the Police Authority. Following interview they appointed me as Assistant Chief Constable with effect from 1st January 1982, so our family didn't have to move again. I was the first member of my SCC to be selected as a Chief Officer.

Chief Officers in Derbyshire shared key responsibilities, such as weekend duty cover and authorising the issue of firearms. Alf Parrish, the new Chief Constable, had only minimal professional experience at both ACC and DCC level and had never actually attended a Police Authority Meeting prior to his appointment as Chief. To cover his own lack of experience, took the full Chief Officer team with him to every Authority Meeting, authorising us to speak to any agenda items which came within our particular spheres of responsibility. He also informed me and my fellow ACC that we would exchange roles after twelve months to broaden our own experience.

Between 1977 and 1981 Derbyshire County Council had been Conservative controlled and Parrish was appointed by that administration. Unfortunately for him, one of its members had been unwise enough to blurt out that they had better hurry up and appoint their own Chief Constable before Labour regained power. Although Parrish was of a conservative disposition, he had no knowledge of what had been said. Nevertheless he suffered because of it when Labour came to power. He was never given a chance and was labelled from the outset as a creature of the Tories.

Before the election the Labour leader, Councillor David Bookbinder, had made it clear that he intended to curtail the autonomy of all county council chief officers. He reminded them that policy is made by elected representatives and the role of chief officers is to provide relevant professional advice and then to implement the policy, whether or not they agree with it. Although a Chief Constable is not legally a local government chief officer, a clash became inevitable and Parrish's own personality, his lack of experience and his political naivety ensured there could only be one winner. The other Chief Officers, including me, had been appointed by the Labour administration so were never subject to the same degree of personal animosity. Between 1981 and 1984 Councillor Bookbinder changed the chair of the Police Authority three times, perhaps an indication that he felt the chair might 'go native' by remaining too long in post.

During this same period a number of other overtly right-wing Chief Constables were experiencing difficulties with their Labour controlled Police Authorities or were at personal loggerheads with their chairpersons (Merseyside, Greater Manchester and Humberside, inter alia) although none of them were quite as inexperienced and politically naïve as Parrish.

One of my proudest achievements as ACC was to secure approval for Doctor Mike Chatterton, a criminologist from Manchester University, to carry out research into police activities and organisational constraints. It was harder to convince colleagues to agree to allow him access than it was to persuade the Police Authority that they had nothing to lose and much to gain from informed research. Mike later acknowledged to me that being granted access had rescued his research career from stagnation.

In January 1984, ACC Ron Hadfield and I exchanged responsibilities as arranged and I took over the Operations role. My first major task was to define our response to the industrial dispute between the National Coal Board (NCB) and the National Union of Mineworkers (NUM). At that time the NCB was the largest employer in Derbyshire. Both the NCB and the NUM were organised into locally autonomous areas, but their borders did not coincide and, to make matters worse, they criss-crossed local authority and police boundaries which didn't help when trying to determine a co-ordinated response. Derbyshire police, therefore, had to relate to three different management teams for the NCB and three different local executive committees for the NUM.

In the absence of a national ballot, each NUM area had voted separately and the results varied considerably. Most of Derbyshire's collieries were located in the North Derbyshire NUM area where the vote produced a majority of sixteen in favour of remaining at work. The executive committee overturned the ballot result and called its members out on strike, a call which they heeded. The collieries at Creswell and Bolsover, although in the county of Derbyshire, belonged to Nottinghamshire NUM and voted heavily to remain at work. The South Derbyshire NUM area included pits in Derbyshire and Leicestershire and over ninety per cent voted to remain at work. So, with just three pits working, two in the north and one in the south, the first week of the dispute was handled by cancelling rest days and placing the whole force on twelve hour shifts. The beginning of week two saw hundreds of pickets from South Yorkshire arrive outside the three working collieries. By the end of that week picket numbers had risen to more than five thousand and it became clear that something would have to be done as the total strength of Derbyshire police was only 1,767 officers. Mutual aid had to be sought simply to deal with the scale of picketing, which meant that police were always outnumbered by five to one.

We met as a chief officer team to discuss the way forward. As it appeared likely that the dispute could last for some time, I argued for clear guidelines on policy and tactics to be published. I also persuaded my colleagues to let me take the lead on the understanding that I would keep them fully informed. They agreed and endorsed the following principles on which our approach to policing the dispute would be based:

1. Derbyshire police is not a party to this dispute. Our role is to preserve the peace and, if necessary, to deal with breaches of the criminal law.
2. The police will take no action in respect of secondary picketing

as it is a civil offence. If secondary picketing occurs it is up to the NCB to seek a legal remedy through the courts.
3. Local communities are already divided so we have to bear in mind the need for their support both now and after the dispute has ended. To that end a Derbyshire officer *must* always be in command at each location to ensure local accountability and consistency of action. Senior officers accompanying mutual aid detachments will be limited to a liaison or welfare role.
4. Picketing numbers alone will not cause the police to intervene, crowd behaviour will be the principal determinant for action. Facilities *must* always be granted for NUM representatives to do what the law permits, i.e. peacefully communicate their views.
5. The police will do nothing to prevent Derbyshire NUM members from moving freely within their own county to exercise their rights under the law.
6. Although protective equipment must be available, it is not to be deployed without chief officer permission. Police dogs will *not* be used to confront picket lines.

Those guidelines were then disseminated throughout the force and divisional commanders and heads of departments were given every opportunity to propose amendments, so there was no lack of understanding at all senior levels.

Every Sunday evening, when fresh mutual aid detachments arrived, I personally briefed their Inspectors and senior officers on our policy guidelines and any changes to the local situation. Mutual aid was provided in multiples of Police Support Units (PSUs), made up of one Inspector, two sergeants and twenty constables. The effectiveness of visiting PSUs depended almost entirely on the quality of their Inspectors, so I asked the National Reporting Centre (NRC) to try to allocate units to us each week from the same forces to maintain continuity in the style of policing, the Devon and Cornwall Constabulary being the best example. Only on one occasion did I have cause to return mutual aid PSUs to their home force on grounds of indiscipline and misbehaviour.

I regularly briefed the chair of the Police Authority who, as an NUM member, was on strike and escorted him round the picket lines to see things for himself. This proved crucial in countering allegations of police misconduct and political bias. I also had regular meetings with members of the North Derbyshire NUM executive committee to which Tony Benn, the MP for Chesterfield, was later invited to attend. Despite having recorded our meetings without permission, he misquoted me in his book 'The Benn Diaries' by claiming that I scapegoated the Metropolitan Police to make things easier for Derbyshire officers after the dispute was over. This was the complete opposite of what I had said. Sadly, Tony Benn had a tendency to disregard anything which challenged his own interpretation of events.

At one of my meetings with senior NCB management, Ian McGregor, the NCB chairman was present. He was a nasty little man, a bully and full of his own importance who accused me of failing to enforce the law in respect of secondary picketing. He didn't take kindly to being reminded that it was a civil, not a criminal, offence and that it was for him to seek a legal remedy through the courts. He threatened that he would get the Home Office to sack me. Shortly afterwards I did receive a telephone call from a very senior official at the Home Office complaining that the Derbyshire Constabulary's policy was too soft and needed toughening up. When I asked him under what authority and on what basis he was making that statement he hung up. One of the sad lessons I learned was that whilst we could always rely on NUM officials to adhere to an agreement once it had been made, the same could not be said for agreements reached with NCB management.

Later in the dispute I escorted HMIC around the picket lines and arranged for him to meet and speak to Derbyshire officers and to PSUs on mutual aid. I also conducted the Archbishop of Canterbury, the Right Reverend Robert Runcie, on a similar tour when he spoke to both pickets and police officers at several sites. He was particularly fascinated to meet and speak to a number of Derbyshire police officers who had close family members on strike whose dependants were being supported by their police overtime payments.

Every day I visited as many colliery sites as possible, with sometimes amusing results. Early one morning I arrived at Pleasley colliery to find about two thousand pickets being confronted by several hundred police officers. Most of the police were from Sussex on mutual aid to

Nottinghamshire who had not realised they had strayed over the border into Derbyshire. As the temperature on both sides appeared to be rising, I ordered the Sussex officers to return to Nottinghamshire and leave me to deal with the situation. Reluctantly they departed, leaving me with just a handful of my own people. One of the NUM officials had a loud hailer, so I borrowed it and the two of us climbed up on to a wall to address the crowd. I told them who I was, explained what had happened and the NUM official confirmed what I had said. We exchanged views about the political situation for quite some time for all to hear, concluding with a debate about what Marx really meant when he used the term alienation. There was no trouble, no violence, no arrests and the crowd dispersed quietly in good humour.

The dispute not only affected me professionally, but also had an impact on my private life. As the strike went on, more and more miners' families found themselves in financial difficulties and the clergy from churches across Derbyshire started to collect and distribute food for those families, reminding me of the actions of our South African friends in London. At a stewards' meeting at my own church I proposed that we participate arguing that, regardless of any personal views about the merits or otherwise of the strike, as Christians we could not stand by and let innocent children go hungry. My fellow stewards agreed to consult the congregation. After the Sunday morning service, the members present were not prepared to commit the church and said it should be left to each individual's conscience to decide whether or not to participate. Later that evening I received a phone call at home from a journalist with a national newspaper asking me why, as the officer in charge of policing the dispute in Derbyshire, I had abrogated police neutrality and was now supporting the strike. He told me that he had received a call from a member of my church alleging that I was a communist and unfit to hold my position. A friend had warned me in advance that another church member was going to surreptitiously tape the proceedings so I had taken great care about what I said at the meeting. I also knew, therefore, who had made the call to the press. I explained to the journalist what had occurred, making it clear that I would take immediate legal action if the story ever went to print; it did not. I gave a similar warning to the person who had made the call about the consequences of repeating his slanderous allegations. That he should act in such a manner was hurtful but not completely surprising, knowing his political views.

The problems for the force caused by NCB/NUM dispute were exacerbated by the opening of a formal investigation into allegations that the Chief Constable had improperly incurred expenditure on building works at HQ without budgetary approval. An enquiry by the district auditor was opened, the Chief Constable was suspended from duty and the DCC was appointed acting Chief.

Chapter Sixteen

Transfer to Sussex Police

In September 1984 the post of DCC in Sussex was advertised and I decided to apply. It was usual to ask the Chief Constable and Chair of the Police Authority to provide references, but in my case it was rather difficult as the Chief was suspended from duty and the Chair was on strike. To get round the problem I asked Derbyshire's Lord Lieutenant and the Bishop of Derby to give their support. I was short-listed but was asked at interview why I had bypassed my Chief and Chairman. I was able to explain the rather unusual circumstances in which I found myself to the authority's satisfaction. One member observed that my CV had mentioned my Christian faith and asked how I reconciled that faith with my policing responsibilities as the two must conflict at times. I replied that he either had a mistaken view of what it is to be a Christian or failed to appreciate what it means to be a police officer. As both are concerned with a search for the truth, they are entirely compatible. He did not ask any further questions. After the interview I was offered the position and accepted.

We sold our house in Swanwick very quickly and moved temporarily into a flat at Sussex Police HQ until we could find a property of our own. Debra had already left home whilst in Derbyshire so, for the very first time, she did not move with us. Stuart, who had begun a civilian traineeship in scenes of crime in Derbyshire, transferred to Sussex Police but in a different department. After a couple of months we bought a house in the village of Kingston near Lewes. There was no Methodist church in Lewes, so we transferred our membership to Dorset Gardens Methodist church in Brighton.

The Sussex Chief Constable, Roger Birch, handed me a political hot potato in my very first week. As ACC (Operations) in Derbyshire I had refused to certify that the accommodation we had provided for Sussex PSUs whilst on mutual aid was sub-standard and therefore blocked the additional payments claimed by officers billeted there. As DCC, under pressure from my new Chief and Police Authority, I had to persuade Derbyshire to reverse that decision in order to balance the Sussex budget, as the officers involved had already been paid (without proper authority). The only other option would have been to require them to reimburse the overpayment, not a good start for me. I managed to convince the Derbyshire finance officer to concede on the grounds that central government would meet the full cost and his own budget would not suffer. During my visits to police stations to introduce myself and get a feel for my new force, I was frequently greeted with the comment, "We've met before Boss, I was in the PSUs you threw out of Derbyshire."

The next task I was given arose out of the IRA bombing of the Grand Hotel, Brighton in October 1984 in an attempt to murder the Prime Minister, Mrs Thatcher, and her cabinet whilst attending the Conservative Party Conference. The Chief asked me to carry out an investigation into the organisational structure of Sussex Police to ascertain whether or not internal failings might have contributed in any way to the IRA's success. I identified a number of structural weaknesses and recommended some organisational changes, but was able to conclude that they had not been contributory factors. McGee, the convicted IRA bomber, later offered the consolation, "You have to be lucky all the time. We only have to be lucky once."

Roger Birch had been appointed CC about a year before I arrived and was not pleased with what he discovered on his arrival. He asked me to review the force management structure to achieve a more corporate approach to decision making. He stressed that divisional commanders and heads of departments must fully understand the implications of the financial constraints imposed on police by both central and local government and accept collective responsibility for their implementation. My review, therefore, focused on establishing clear lines of accountability, operational and financial, and the willingness to learn from well managed non-police organisations in both the public and private sectors. Value for money became the byword. Police officers were gradually removed from administrative duties to be replaced by qualified civil staff. A programme to civilianise functions not requiring the possession of full police powers was commenced, starting with fingerprints and photography followed by scenes of crime. The Sussex Police Federation chairman publicly accused me of civilianising scenes of crime in order to find a job for my son Stuart, who had applied for one of the new trainee posts. He later apologised (privately).

Some relatively quick results were needed to show what could be done. By disbanding the Mounted and Marine sections I was able to convince the Police Authority to use their respective budgets to purchase a helicopter which provided greater cover far more quickly and efficiently than they had ever managed between them. In my first three years reductions in paperwork and reallocating responsibilities delivered time savings equivalent to returning two hundred officers to operational duties at minimal additional cost.

Shortly after my appointment as DCC I received a request for an interview from BBC Radio Sussex. At the end of the interview the station manager asked me if I had any previous experience of local radio, so I told him about my time on Radio Derby. He later contacted me, having spoken to his colleague in Derby, and asked whether or not I would be willing to do something similar on Radio Sussex. I agreed and once again took part in presenting 'Thought for the Day'.

A barrister acquaintance invited me to become a member of the 'Society for the Reform of Criminal Law.' The majority of the Society's members were either lawyers and/or academics from countries within the Common Law tradition with very strong representation in Australia and Canada. British members were trying to broaden the Society's membership, hence my invitation. I accepted and for a number of years attended annual conferences and delivered papers on current legal issues, the most memorable being in the Sydney Opera House where I led a discussion following my paper on the problems of policing public order in a democratic society. I also addressed plenary sessions at the annual conferences of the British Sociological Association and the Howard League for Penal Reform.

In December, 1985, Arab terrorists launched attacks with grenades and assault rifles on passengers waiting to board flights to Israel at

Rome and Vienna airports, killing nineteen people and wounding over a hundred. On learning of the attacks I immediately instructed the officer in charge of policing Gatwick Airport to visit both locations and speak to his opposite numbers there without delay to find out exactly what had occurred and what lessons we could learn from the incidents. None of the other British forces responsible for policing our international airports contacted Rome or Vienna or spoke to those who had been involved for first-hand accounts of the attacks and the effectiveness of their response. Instead, the Metropolitan and Greater Manchester Police made front-page news by arming their officers at Heathrow and Ringway Airports with automatic weapons without consulting fellow Chief Officers or even informing them. Hitherto British police at airports had only been issued with handguns. One of the key findings made by my Gatwick commander was that, although both the Italian and Austrian police had been armed with both automatic weapons and side-arms, they had discarded their sub-machine guns in favour of their hand guns as being more appropriate for use in an airport terminal crowded with passengers. The terrorists killed by police and El Al security officers were shot with hand guns. In 1986 the forces responsible for policing Heathrow and Gatwick airports together with the ACPO President were asked to give evidence about airport security to a Parliamentary Committee at the House of Commons. I related what we in Sussex had done and stressed the importance of basing major changes to policing policy on solid evidence rather than knee-jerk reactions. On first entering the room I noticed that one of the MPs on the Committee had been a contemporary of mine at the LSE. He had obviously recognised me but was reminded of Parliamentary protocol by the committee chairman when he greeted me by my Christian name.

 I learned a great deal from Roger Birch about what it takes to be a good Chief Constable. Once he had satisfied himself that I was capable, he left the day to day running of the force to me, freeing him to pursue his national and international interests. Right from the start he told me that my most important job was to tell him all the things other people were too frightened to say and, above all, to tell him the things he didn't want to hear. I had to prevent him from doing anything that was either improper or unwise, particularly in respect of finance. I gave instructions to the force finance officer to do the same for me, thinking back to what had happened to Alf Parrish in Derbyshire.

Having been a successful candidate through the EI process for both the Special Course and the Senior Command Course, I was delighted when I was invited to join the panel of EI assessors, first for the Graduate Entry Scheme and then the Senior Command Course.

After three years of running the force I felt ready to take on the next rank and applied for the newly advertised post of Chief Constable of Hampshire. I was called for interview and felt that it had gone really well. The Police Authority panel withdrew to make its decision and surprisingly kept all the applicants waiting in suspense for over an hour and a half for their decision. They finally returned to announce that Hampshire's DCC was the successful candidate. The chairman then asked to speak me in private. He was extremely embarrassed and explained that the panel had unanimously agreed that I was by far the best candidate, but they couldn't disappoint their own Deputy by not appointing him. It was difficult to restrain myself from asking if that was the case why they had subjected us all to such a charade. "Never mind" he said "You'll soon get a Chief's job with your track record." That was not much consolation, but little did I realise that it would become the first of a number of similar occasions.

I continued to apply for Chief Constable vacancies and received consistent support from Roger Birch, HMIC and Sussex Police Authority, although in the latter case the support was tempered with the phrase, "Although he is not one of us ……." an observation on my politics from a Conservative councillor in Sussex to one in another county.

I was awarded the Queen's Police Medal (QPM) in 1987. Despite being a long term opponent of the British honours system, I accepted in the knowledge that the QPM can only be awarded to a police officer, so financial donations or political favours play no part in the recommendation. Mum was delighted to attend the ceremony at Police HQ along with Kathleen, Stuart and his wife Louise, when the Lord Lieutenant of East Sussex presented me with my medal.

Towards the end of 1989 the Velvet Revolution took place in Czechoslovakia when one of the most hard-line communist regimes in Europe was peacefully overthrown. The new government appealed to the UK for help in restructuring and retraining its police, following which I was asked by the Foreign and Commonwealth Office (FCO) to visit Czechoslovakia to assess what needed to be done. I selected a small team in which Chief Superintendent Colin Moore from Devon & Cornwall and Superintendent Mike Bowron from Sussex were my immediate choices. The final place was more difficult to fill as I was advised to include someone who was not only a Czech speaker but also had some knowledge of British policing. That advice was invaluable and my dilemma was resolved when a colleague recommended a serving officer in the Essex force who had been born in Prague, Police Constable Jan Vaclav (John) Mertl. Before our first visit I was briefed by Czech specialists from the FCO and also by members of the Secret Intelligence Service (SIS), although both organisations claimed that things were moving so fast that they knew little about what was actually happening on the ground and would I please update them on my return.

PC Mertl's worth was demonstrated during our first visit to Prague when he warned me that the interpreters provided by our hosts were not correctly translating what we had said. Their difficulties seemed to stem from the fact that they had no knowledge about the police of either country and did not understand some of the professional terminology. We managed to resolve the problem without too much embarrassment or causing a diplomatic incident. My report was accepted by both the FCO for the UK and by the Federal Ministry of the Interior for the Czechoslovak government as the basis for a long term project and we were asked to return to carry out further research.

Investigation for HMIC & PCA

In the summer of 1990 I was asked by HMIC to undertake an investigation, supervised by the Police Complaints Authority (PCA), into alleged misconduct by ACC Halford of the Merseyside Police. I informed HMIC that Alison Halford had been one of the two female officers on my Special Course at Bramshill in 1966, but I had neither served with her nor spoken to her since then, although I had followed her career with interest. He confirmed there was no potential conflict of interest. I chose a Detective Superintendent and a Detective Sergeant from Sussex to assist and we travelled to Liverpool for a briefing.

Merseyside's DCC outlined the details of the alleged misconduct and also informed me that ACC Halford had lodged a complaint against Merseyside Police for sex discrimination. The DCC asked that I keep him up to date with the progress of my investigation. I made it clear that my responsibility was to the PCA, not to Merseyside Police and asked for full co-operation and disclosure of any relevant material held by the force.

The investigation itself was relatively straightforward. Witnesses were interviewed, evidence was gathered and I kept my supervisor at the PCA fully informed. I interviewed ACC Halford twice in the presence of her legal representative. She denied the allegations and claimed that my enquiry had been deliberately instigated in order to damage her sex discrimination case against Merseyside Police.

Sadly, I didn't always get the co-operation I had requested from the force. Some members had to be treated as though they were hostile witnesses and the information I was given was not always reliable. Our office accommodation was searched and a locked desk was forced open, causing us to move to a more secure location. Instances of divided loyalties caused real problems for some officers who felt that ACC Halford had been badly treated by the force but probably had done whatever had been alleged. On the other hand her lawyers always seemed to know in advance what I and my team were doing.

I was later told by the Chief HMIC that it was my well-known commitment to gender equality and political sensitivity which had caused me to be chosen as investigating officer. In my report I drew a clear distinction between certain salacious allegations and the more substantive area of professional negligence, which I found to be proved beyond doubt. My PCA supervisor signed off the report and authorised me to present it to the Police Authority. The Merseyside Authority was known to be as divided as the force, with both supporters and opponents of ACC Halford already having gone public with their views. Unfortunately the Police Authority had a reputation for leaking like a sieve, so I had to control the distribution of my report with great care. Each Authority member received a personal advance copy to be returned after the meeting. To make premature disclosure more difficult, I included a means of identifying the origin of any leaked copies. I informed members of what I had done and there were no leaks. I presented my report to the Police Authority and took questions from members for over an hour. My recommendations were accepted and ACC Halford's suspension from duty was authorised. Legally, the Authority's Clerk should have informed Miss Halford of her suspension but he chickened out and left it to me, which was not a pleasant experience. She turned on me in a rage using the foulest language and refused to surrender her warrant card.

Unexpected Developments

Perhaps naively I supposed that to be the end of the matter, but soon afterwards received a call from Sir John Woodcock, Chief HMIC, asking me to come to his office in London. There he informed me that tape recordings of ACC Halford's office telephone at Merseyside Police HQ had been brought to his attention as they indicated that she might have suborned a member of the PCA in order to thwart my investigation. I was then asked to carry out a separate enquiry into allegations of potentially unlawful conduct and collusion between a member of the PCA and ACC Halford. Given the importance of maintaining public confidence in the integrity of the PCA, I was to report to the Director of Public Prosecutions (DPP) in person and no-one else. Some of the tape recordings included conversations between ACC Halford and her legal representatives, therefore the tapes would be edited by a barrister of Queen's Counsel (QC) standing to remove any privileged material. I was subsequently briefed by the DPP in his office where the said QC handed over the edited recordings.

I asked the same Detective Superintendent to work with me again and together we reviewed the edited tapes. Conversations relevant to our enquiry were between ACC Halford and a male member of the PCA. It quickly became clear that the two had a close, possibly sexual, relationship. ACC Halford had asked him to find out from my supervisor at the PCA what progress my investigation was making and then pass the information to her, which he did. As soon as I was satisfied that a strong 'prima facie' case had been established I requested a private interview with the PCA chairman, Judge Peter. He saw me in his office where I outlined the nature of my investigation and the DPP's worry that the integrity of the PCA might have been compromised. His response shook me to the core. Instead of concern that a member of his staff might be corrupt or had been corrupted, he focussed on the method of acquisition of the evidence. The tape recordings, he said, must have been illegally obtained, therefore their contents were inadmissible; end of story. I took no pleasure in disabusing him of that notion and correcting him in law. I emphasised that my visit was a courtesy call only and I would be interviewing his staff member under caution on suspicion of having committed a criminal offence or offences.

The PCA member was interviewed under caution and admitted everything quite freely, including his emotional relationship with ACC Halford. He had known her for some time through her role as ACC Personnel in Merseyside and had developed a high regard for her. He felt she had been badly treated by her force and considered that he had done nothing wrong. My own PCA supervisor was horrified to learn of his colleague's duplicity and of Judge Peter's reaction. My report to the DPP recommended that both the PCA member and ACC Halford be prosecuted, inter alia, for conspiracy to pervert the course of justice, but the DPP ruled that it would not be in the public interest so to do. The PCA staff member was placed on 'gardening leave' and his contract was not renewed. No further action was taken against ACC Halford and Public Interest Immunity was invoked in respect of my report, so it was never published.

In 1990 I was approached by an international recruitment agency and asked to consider applying for the post of Commissioner of the New South Wales Police in Australia. Their offer included business class travel and a two week stay in Sydney for Kathleen and me, all expenses paid with no strings attached. Tempting as though the offer was, I could not in all conscience accept, as I had no desire to move to Australia. I therefore declined the offer.

Chapter Seventeen

Transfer to Humberside

I continued to seek promotion and early in 1991 applied for two newly advertised vacancies for Chief Constables, the first in Northumbria and the second in Humberside. Shortly after submitting my applications Kathleen suffered a serious back injury whilst at home and was admitted to hospital. The immediate prognosis was not good. The consultant expressed concern that she could have suffered permanent damage to her spine and might not be able to walk again. With that initial diagnosis in mind I withdrew both applications, explaining my reasons and came to terms with remaining in Sussex as DCC.

Two months later I received a letter from the Clerk to the Humberside Police Authority stating that their Chief's post was to be re-advertised and did I wish to be considered. Kathleen had been discharged from hospital and fortunately had made a good recovery. We talked it over and decided I should re-apply. There was no internal candidate and I was offered the job. Following the interview I had a series of meetings with the Chief Executive of Humberside County Council and Clerk to the Police Authority, for a briefing on past and current political problems within the county and the absence of good relations between the retiring Chief and the Police Authority, particularly with its chairman. Following those meetings I invited the chair and vice chair of the Humberside Police Authority to visit Sussex to see how things could be done differently when officers and elected members work closely together for the benefit of the local community.

Domestically this move did not proceed as smoothly as on previous occasions. We were unable to sell our house in Kingston for quite some time, so Kathleen remained in Sussex whilst I began my new life in

Humberside. I lived in single accommodation at Hessle Police Station for six months until the house was sold and then rented a property in Beverly for us to be together whilst we searched for a permanent home. We eventually bought a house in Kirk Ella on the outskirts of the city of Hull. The village had a small Methodist chapel within walking distance of our new home, so we were well suited.

Local Background

The county of Humberside had been created in 1974 as part of a restructuring of local authorities by Edward Heath's Conservative government. It comprised the former East Riding of Yorkshire, the City of Kingston upon Hull and the Lindsey area of Lincolnshire. Political, historical and cultural rivalries still existed despite the passage of time and the opening of the Humber Bridge to link both sides of the river. For the greater part of its existence the county council had been Labour controlled.

My predecessor was Chief Constable from 1976 until 1991. If asked "To whom are you accountable?" his response was "The Queen and the Home Secretary." Most of his formative service had been in the Metropolitan Police when the Home Secretary had been its Police Authority. He had no time for elected Police Authorities and even less for Labour politicians, particularly at local level. It was little wonder, therefore, that his period of office was marked by constant conflict, except for the years between 1977 and 1981, when the Conservatives controlled the county council.

In 1984 he had been President of ACPO and, in my view, became too close to government ministers during the miners' strike. His political sympathies were on the right and he overtly socialised with leading Conservative councillors, acknowledging them as personal friends. A state of almost open warfare had led the Police Authority to fill vacancies at DCC and ACC level with candidates of whom he did not approve, none of whom were graduates of the Senior Command Course. He was an instinctive traditionalist and mistrusted policies requiring gender, racial or sexual equality. The internal command structure was extremely hierarchical with decision making tightly controlled from the centre. HMIC warned me that I had inherited the weakest leadership team in the country.

In fairness I must add that my predecessor was kindness itself personally in welcoming Kathleen and me to Humberside and, as he intended to remain in the area, he made me a promise that he would never publicly comment on any decision I might make as Chief. If he felt that I was making a mistake he would speak to me personally and not to the press. He was as good as his word and I respected him for that.

Change and Reform
All of this meant that I had a series of critical issues to address from my first day in office, with no time to settle in gradually. I had to put an end to conflict with the Police Authority and County Council and drag a reluctant force into the late twentieth century. An early assessment of my ACPO colleagues was that the DCC was professionally competent but I was unsure where his loyalties lay; the ACC (Admin) had raised incompetence to a completely new high, but the ACC (Operations) showed promise as a Chief Officer. The Police Authority had imposed a civilian accountant on the force with a salary at Assistant Chief level. My predecessor had exiled him to a separate building and refused to accept him as a fellow chief officer. His financial acumen and administrative skills were desperately needed to compensate for weaknesses in the rest of the command team, so I immediately welcomed him as a full member and moved him into an office in the command corridor.

I accepted an invitation from the County Council's Chief Executive to attend his weekly chief officer meetings to emphasise that policing is an integral part of local public sector service provision. I also chose to attend the full County Council meetings, sitting in uniform alongside council chief officers for all to see. The former CC had always refused to attend such meetings, even under the Conservatives.

The Chair of the Police Authority was a young man of twenty-nine and openly gay. At our first pre-agenda meeting I made a point of sitting next to him, which my predecessor could never bring himself to do, and suggested that he and his vice-chair might like to meet regularly with me and the Authority's clerk to discuss problems, prevent misunderstandings and improve relations. I also asked for his support in addressing a number of internal force policy changes directed towards improving equal opportunities. It took him completely by surprise as he had assumed that I had not been honest when I said I would do this at my job interview.

I arranged meetings with the leaders of the three main political parties on the County Council to introduce myself and explain how I hoped that things were going to change. My aim was not just to make a number of symbolic, albeit important, gestures but to send a clear public message that Humberside Police was under new management and that I had every intention of continuing in the way in which I had started.

One of my earliest decisions was to order the closure of all bars in police stations, which seemed to me to involve double standards. Whilst members of the public were being prosecuted for drink-drive offences, police officers were consuming alcohol during mid-shift meal breaks and at the completion of duty before driving home. I drew a clear distinction between bars in operational police stations and those in police sporting and social clubs on separate premises. I also let it be known that any police officer appearing before a disciplinary tribunal having been convicted in court of a drink-drive offence would be dismissed.

Humberside CID was obsessed by detection rates and blatantly manipulated the crime statistics to make the force appear more efficient than it was. Criminals were visited in prison and persuaded to admit responsibility for undetected crimes similar to those for which they had been convicted, whether or not they had actually committed them. The practice served no other purpose than to fiddle the figures; no undetected crimes were truly solved, no property was recovered and restored to its owner and no victims had the satisfaction of knowing a criminal was now behind bars and unable to prey upon others. The system was so corrupt that up to forty per cent of the detection rate came from that source alone. Each division had two or three detectives engaged full time on this technique, known as 'prison visit write-offs' which was itself a recognised category in the official Home Office statistics. Not only did it create a false impression of police effectiveness, but it took away resources from the actual investigation of crime. It undermined the integrity of the force and potentially weakened public confidence. I was heartened to learn that the Chief of Northumbria Police was also considering ways of dealing with the same problem. We agreed to coordinate our approach.

I was aware that in stopping the practice I would face a great deal of opposition, both internal and external, so I started to look for potential allies. I expressed my concerns to HMIC who offered his personal support but hinted that both politicians and civil servants at the Home Office were only concerned with the final figures, not how they had been achieved. He commented that they would be most unhappy to see a fall in the detection rate. I then consulted the chair and leading members of the Police Authority. They too were initially reluctant to see a drop in the detection rate, although they sympathised with my position. Eventually they agreed to back me in public and try to divert responsibility on to the Conservative Home Secretary for knowing of the problem but doing nothing about it. It didn't help that some of them saw it as another way to get back at my predecessor. My final call was to the editor of the Hull Daily Mail, a widely read and highly influential local newspaper. I knew that many detectives regularly briefed the local press, so I wanted him to hear my side of the story first.

Although the CID didn't like the change, it didn't develop into a real issue locally until two years later when the Home Office published league tables of police forces showing Humberside at the bottom for crime detection. But for my earlier intervention, the Hull Daily Mail's headline might have been far worse. Ironically the force praised by the Home Office for its success in tackling crime was using the same technique of manipulation that I had banned.

I learned from the FCO that the Czechoslovak Federal Government was so pleased with my report on their police that they had asked for my team to be allowed to continue its work. I sought and gained Police Authority approval to continue, including a commitment to host Czech and Slovak police officers, civil servants and politicians in Humberside. We visited two or three times per year until 1999, embarking upon a series of joint projects, particularly after the dissolution of the federal state and the creation of the independent Czech and Slovak Republics. The success of this work led to my being called to give evidence to Lord Patten's Committee of Enquiry into the future of policing in Northern Ireland, with particular reference to the importance of making a clean break with the past and the symbolism of new titles and uniforms. I actually recommended to him that the Royal Ulster Constabulary be renamed the

Police Service of Northern Ireland (PSNI) and be given a new uniform, both of which he accepted and recommended to HM Government.

The response by the Czech and Slovak governments to the work carried out by my team led me to consider using the information we had gathered as an academic case study in its own right. I submitted a research proposal to the Faculty of Politics at Hull University which was accepted, following which I registered with the faculty as a part-time doctoral student.

Internal force changes focused on team building, devolving responsibility and accountability and modernising personnel policies. Equal opportunities was placed at the forefront of all personnel practices and assessment centres replaced the former system for selecting candidates for promotion. Staff associations for police officers and trades unions for civil staff became more closely involved in the change process with consequent improvements in morale. I continued with my role as an assessor for the EI process and encouraged more Humberside officers to put themselves forward as candidates. Several did so and were successful in both attending the SCC and subsequently gaining chief officer appointments.

Improved relations with the Police Authority led to regular joint broadcasts with the Authority's Chair on Radio Humberside phone-in programmes to answer questions from the public on policing and other local issues. We also achieved all party support in opposing the Conservative government's proposals to diminish the democratic relevance of Police Authorities by imposing on them so-called 'independent' members.

In seeking to place Humberside Police at the heart of local community life, regular meetings were arranged with local MPs, MEPs and faith leaders. The MPs refused to meet other parties and would only attend with members of their own political group. Church and faith leaders were less tribal and welcomed the opportunity to raise issues of concern and discuss local problems.

When the Boundary Commission visited Humberside to take local soundings on the future of the county, I gave oral evidence in favour of keeping Humberside as a county in its own right. My sole caveat was that, should the Commission recommend the abolition of the county, then the three emergency services of Police, Fire and Ambulance should be retained as county wide organisations retaining the Humberside name. Despite fierce and frantic lobbying by local and national Conservative politicians, the argument was accepted and implemented.

Investigation at Request of HMIC

I was asked on a number of occasions to conduct investigations in other force areas, none of which were particularly high profile or attracted much public interest. But in 1996 it seemed as though history was about to repeat itself. I received a call from HMIC asking me to examine the case of a female officer in Lincolnshire who had commenced proceedings against her force for sexual discrimination and had then been charged with disciplinary offences and suspended from duty. Was this to be the Halford case all over again?

HMIC was very explicit; this was a highly charged and delicately balanced political situation involving three forces. At the Lincolnshire Chief's request, a Nottinghamshire team had begun an enquiry into the female officer's conduct. However, the officer leading the investigation felt that he had been subjected to such a degree of improper pressure by the Lincolnshire Chief that he terminated his enquiry and refused to continue. The Nottinghamshire Chief Constable was so aggrieved by this that he referred the matter to HMIC who had now turned to me. He asked me to review whatever evidence the aborted Nottinghamshire enquiry had managed to assemble, to speak to the investigating officer and report back, keeping my actions as low key as possible. He would then decide what to do.

I did as requested, finding the Nottinghamshire officer to be an experienced, honest and entirely credible senior investigator who had uncovered more than enough to warrant further action. His unfinished report seriously questioned the validity of the original decision by Lincolnshire Police to charge the officer under the Discipline Code. I reported back and HMIC confirmed what I had suspected all along, that he wanted me to conduct an investigation into the actions of the Lincolnshire Chief himself. I asked for, and received, clear terms of reference, selected a team to assist me and briefed them, stressing the need for absolute confidentiality. HMIC said that he would inform

Lincolnshire's Police Authority of the reasons for my investigation and would warn them not interfere or comment publicly, a message significant in itself. Members would receive my report in due course when any further action would be their responsibility.

The investigation necessarily required me and my team to visit Lincolnshire HQ to interview not only the Chief Constable but anyone else who might have relevant information. I spoke to the Chief in his office, informing him of my terms of reference and asked him to nominate someone to act as a liaison officer to provide whatever documentation I required and arrange access to personnel and premises. Our conversation was difficult as he bitterly resented HMIC's involvement, which he described as unwarranted interference. Nevertheless he nominated his DCC for the liaison role. I was delighted with his choice as the DCC was an officer whom I knew to be a man of complete integrity.

It was difficult to get Lincolnshire personnel to open up as many of them were afraid of their Chief, whose personal style could only be described as bullying. He ruled by fear and was known to be vindictive. I used the incomplete report by Nottinghamshire as a starting point but had my team re-interview everyone to enable us to draw our own conclusions. I interviewed the female officer myself to hear her story and to make a personal assessment of her credibility. Part of my insistence that we work to reach a speedy conclusion was driven by the fact that the Lincolnshire Chief was pressing hard for disciplinary action against the female officer to go ahead, despite my investigation. The feeling in the force was that the officer was bound to be sacked for daring to challenge the Chief, regardless of anything else.

The investigation eventually reached the point at which the team and I were completely satisfied that there was absolutely no case for the female officer to answer and that the Chief's actions had been both oppressive and possibly unlawful. I completed my report, briefed HMIC, and arranged to appear before a panel of the Lincolnshire Police Authority to discuss my findings and answer questions. I explained in great detail what I had found and pulled no punches in describing what I thought of their Chief Constable's unprofessional and intemperate behaviour. Members were extremely defensive and reluctant to hear anything against their Chief, implying that both investigations had been biased from the outset. One member even suggested that I was jealous of their Chief. They had clearly been briefed about the discipline case and were dismissive of the female officer whom they labelled as a troublemaker. I pointed out that they had only heard one side of the story and showed them the limitations of what they had been told. They were shocked when I said that I was so convinced of the female officer's integrity that I had offered her a post in the same rank in my own force and hoped that they would persuade their Chief not to try to block the transfer. Following the submission of my report the Lincolnshire DCC lifted the female officer's suspension and all disciplinary charges were dropped.

I do not know what action, if indeed any, was taken by the Lincolnshire Police Authority, but almost immediately afterwards their Chief Constable retired and was replaced. The female officer did transfer to Humberside, together with her husband, where she enjoyed a successful career, being promoted on two further occasions (by my successors) and winning a national award. In 1998 she settled her case with Lincolnshire Police when the Industrial Tribunal awarded her the sum of £60,000 in damages. Lincolnshire's new Chief Constable offered a full public apology. Once again my report was classified as subject to Public Interest Immunity and was, therefore, never published.

In advising the Czech and Slovak governments, my discussions and meetings with cabinet ministers, senior civil servants and police chiefs had frequently moved beyond the relatively straightforward world of crime, public order and traffic policing into the realm of relationships between central and local government and constitutional issues. "How does your constitution incorporate this or that change?" Or "What does your constitution say about this?" were typical questions. It was not easy for my hosts to come to terms with the fact that their democratic ideal, the United Kingdom, had no written constitution. On the other hand, neither was it always easy for me to explain to them the intricacies of Parliamentary Sovereignty without revealing my own personal opinions.

Back at home I noted that in a letter to 'The Guardian' newspaper the eminent human rights lawyer, Michael Mansfield QC, had criticised the Conservative Government for destroying centuries old rights. I took issue with that and decided to go public with my own views. Following my conversations in the Czech and Slovak Republics I argued that due to the lack of a written constitution, bill of rights and freedom of information legislation, British people had no inalienable rights. They are not citizens but subjects, and only possess transitory rights which can be given by one administration and then taken away by the next. I called for a written constitution, the establishment of a constitutional court and the incorporation of the European Convention on Human Rights into domestic law. Despite some reporting of my comments, I received little public response, for or against. I was heartened that the new Labour government intimated its intention to legislate on both Human Rights and Freedom of Information.

In 1998, after much deliberation and with some reluctance, ACPO Council agreed to create a new committee to oversee research by and into the police and appointed me as its first chairman. Given my track record in opening up policing to serious academic researchers I was gratified by the appointment. My initial intention had been to encourage support for the establishment of a professional policing institute similar to those which exist for other professions, an idea that had been widely canvassed for some years. However, there was considerable opposition to the concept from the other police staff associations, the Superintendents' Association and the Police Federation, which regarded it as both a challenge and a threat. Unfortunately those same misgivings were also articulated by some within ACPO itself. I had hoped that a professional institute could bring together people from inside and outside the service in a non-threatening forum through which issues could be discussed without representative bodies being tied to them. It could even develop into a think tank where controversial subjects could be debated that would be too difficult or delicate to air in existing groups. As chair of the new committee I was granted an 'ex officio' seat on police related committees of the Economic and Social Research Council (ESRC) and hoped that relations between academic researchers and the police service might thereby be improved. Sadly internal opposition to the creation of a policing institute was too strong and it never came to fruition.

Remembering the promise made to me by my predecessor, I assured my successor that I would never publicly comment on anything he did, which I managed to do despite pressure from both local and national media.

Chapter Eighteen

The Next Step - Retirement

Although I could have continued in post until the age of sixty-five, I decided to retire at sixty having achieved almost everything I had set out to do. After eight years in charge, I could confidently leave Humberside Police in a far better state than on my arrival and secure in the hands of a stronger team in every respect. Retirement itself held no fears as my life had never been constrained by the demands of work and I joked that my intention was to draw my pension for longer than I had contributed towards it, as there was so much more to experience and enjoy.

In 1996 I had registered in the Faculty of Politics at Hull University as a part-time PhD student. Drawing on almost nine years' work for the FCO, I used the police in the Czech and Slovak republics as a case study to assess how deeply democratic ideas and practices had become embedded in the two countries after almost fifty years under totalitarian regimes. I submitted my thesis in 2000 and having survived my 'Viva' was awarded my doctorate in 2001.

During my first two years of retirement I continued to act as an unpaid expert for the Council of Europe dealing with Police and Human Rights and Codes of Ethics for the Police in the former Communist states of Bulgaria, Moldova and the Czech and Slovak republics. I was invited to draft a paper for the Council's Parliamentary Committee on 'The Fundamentals of Democratic Policing' which I circulated and then delivered orally in the National Assembly building in Paris, followed by questions from members of that group. It later became one of the source documents used by the Council in formulating its own position on policing a democratic society. I was also invited by the European

Commission to join a multi-national team tasked with assessing the progress made by the Slovak Republic in meeting the standards required for European Union membership in the field of Justice and Home Affairs.

At home I served on the Police Discipline Appeals Panel for a further two years before deciding to draw to a close my involvement with the police. I carried out one final investigation on behalf of the West Yorkshire Police Authority to ascertain whether or not there was any validity to a complaint which had been lodged against its Chief Constable. I was able to reassure the Authority that there was no merit to the allegation and further investigation was unnecessary.

Return to Sussex

After so many moves during our life together, Kathleen and I had intended to remain in Humberside for our retirement. However in 2001 Debra and Stuart, who had both settled in Sussex, asked us to move closer to them for the sake of our grandchildren. We agreed and bought a house in Brighton, equidistant between the two of them. Ironically, only six months after our move, Debra and her family relocated to Hong Kong following her husband's promotion to a senior post there by his employers. Over the following thirteen years we visited Hong Kong eleven times prior to Debra's eventual return to the UK.

Our new home was in the suburb of Patcham, so we initially transferred our membership to Patcham Methodist Church where both Kathleen and I served as Stewards. After some time and much soul-searching we concluded that we were not truly comfortable as members of that particular congregation. We moved back to Dorset Gardens Methodist Church (DGMC) in the city centre where we had worshipped during our previous time in Sussex. DGMC's wholehearted commitment to inclusiveness, acting as a focal point for its local community and providing security and a safe space for vulnerable groups and individuals was and is in complete accord with our vision of Christian service in the twenty-first century. I joined the organists' rota, playing on a regular basis for both morning and evening worship. I was appointed as a Circuit Steward and member of the circuit leadership team serving my full term of six years.

Kathleen and I joined the Patcham branch of the University of the Third Age (U3A) soon after our arrival in Brighton and I served as its Chairman for two years, helping to establish a new U3A branch at nearby Preston Park. Patcham's existing French language groups were already full, so I offered to host a less formal, but more advanced, French conversation group which still meets every two weeks. I provided piano accompaniment for the singing group which gave a number of local concerts both within and outside of U3A. I thoroughly enjoy chairing the bi-monthly discussion on current affairs which usually attracts a good attendance, but takes up a great deal of time in preparation. Our youngest grandson showed me how to put together a powerpoint presentation to add interest to my talks to U3A and other local voluntary groups. I cover a range of topics and enjoy the preparation as much as the actual speaking.

Conclusions

I am satisfied with what I achieved professionally, particularly as I never suffered from a burning desire at an early age to be a police officer. I didn't don my first uniform with the ambition of becoming a Chief Constable and consider myself fortunate to have enjoyed the different aspects of my career. I took advantage of events as they occurred. I have always felt more comfortable with the idea of a police service than a police force. I did take my oath of office as a constable seriously and strove to live up to the promise I made back in January 1962, to treat all people fairly according to the law. It didn't have to be done deliberately, it just came naturally as the right thing to do. My legacy is in the multitude of policies and practices I introduced as a chief officer in three forces to ensure real equality, from initial entry to internal selection procedures and broader personnel issues. If fellow police officers are not treated fairly by their own commanders, how can they be expected to treat the public with fairness? The tone of any organisation is always set from the top.

Writing this autobiography has caused me to reflect and think about what is important in life. Kathleen often remarks that her two favourite words are 'love' and 'home.' Both words resonate with me and always seem to have been at the centre of my existence. When the two of us were children, home had a specific geographical location. After our marriage, however, we had to make our own home and decide what it meant for us as a couple. In moving away from our geographical roots, we defined home as the place where we were together as a family. I loved my parents and I know they loved me, but I did not choose them. Kathleen and I did choose each other and we decided to make our own family. Being together as a family has always been what really matters, regardless of where we found ourselves and we are still a close family, which is why we returned to Brighton. Just like church, home is people, not a building or a place.

My faith has followed a similar developmental route. Belief was important when I was a child, but that is no longer the case and has not been so for many years. My faith does not depend upon doctrine, dogma or belief and I most certainly don't need a creed. It's how I live my life among my fellow human beings that's important, how I relate to them and how I treat them; it's about what I do, not what I claim to believe. Had I to be more specific, I would sum it up in the words of John Wesley, the founder of Methodism;

> 'Do all the **good** you can,
> by all the **means** you can,
> in all the **ways** you can,
> in all the **places** you can,
> at all the **times** you can,
> to all the **people** you can,
> as **long as ever** you can.'

That faith journey has been mirrored in my political development, from middle of the road Labour like my parents, to left-wing socialist. Although I was not allowed to be a member of a political party as a serving police officer, I never tried to hide my political convictions just as I never hid my Christianity, whilst doing my best not to impose either on the people around me. My political ideas flow from my Christian faith. I have voted for the Labour Party (despite its imperfections) at every election since reaching voting age in 1960, from Parish Council to General Election and cannot conceive of changing that practice.

My professional life allowed me the privilege of experiencing and working at the highest level with local and central government under both the Labour and Conservative parties. In helping foreign governments to discover democracy after years of totalitarianism, my socialism has moved from theory to praxis. I've learned that it's more important to ask the right questions than to pretend to have all the answers and, above all, never to forget on whose behalf you are seeking to change society. I have joined the Labour Party and play an active role in my local branch. Recalling Roy Hattersley's put-down of Tony Benn, I sincerely hope that I too will not be deemed to have 'immatured with age.'

Printed in Great Britain
by Amazon